Endorsements

No Matter What is written by a beautiful, tender-hearted, wise, honest, and relatable warrior, Monika. Monika's heart and passion to bring hope and insight are a tremendous asset to everyone seeking to understand the struggles young people are facing. Thank you, Monika, for sharing your heart, life and love with us! We are truly blessed because of you.

—Andrea Fehr
Author, Freedom Coach Keynote Speaker
and Podcaster

No Matter What is an inspiring story of courage, unconditional love, and intuition.

Monika brings to light the struggles teens face today in a world full of outside influence and provides hope for those feeling alone with their pain. She challenges you to fight for your children, never give up on them, and reminds you that your battle is not in vain and is not done alone.

—Lorie Gurnett
Award-winning Author
and Transformational Coach

No Matter What—An extremely authentic and relatable account of a mother's journey of never giving up on her child. The fight between listening to one's intuition vs all the other "opinions," "voices," or judgments is far too familiar for families these days.

Monika's real, raw, and very honest story reminds us regardless of the struggle, we are the experts in our lives.

Thank you, Monika, Samantha, and family, for the vulnerability and having the courage to share your experience with others.

—Angela Hamshire and Christine Vachon
Soul Sisters Memorial Foundation

Raising our children is often arduous and filled with hidden challenges. When your child has special needs, the challenges are greater and sometimes seem insurmountable. In writing, *No Matter What: How Far Would You Go to Save Your Child?*, Monika Polefka-Proulx has shown us how unrelenting parental love can save a child. With honesty and vulnerability, Monika shares the raw truth of the harrowing journey her family endured as they refused to let their daughter get lost in the black hole of the drug culture. The Proulx's faced every parent's worst nightmare, and despite getting only minimal help from the cold, judgmental school system and the powerless legal system, they never gave up. *No Matter What: How Far Would You Go to Save Your Child?* is a one-of-a-kind memoir from a gifted storyteller.

—Marci Brockman
Author and host of the hit podcast
Permission to Heal

No Matter What

How Far Would You Go to Save Your Child?

MONIKA POLEFKA-PROULX

Published by Author Academy Elite
PO Box 43, Powell, OH 43065
www.AuthorAcademyElite.com

Identifiers:

LCCN: 2021910671

ISBN: 978-1-64746-821-7 (paperback)
ISBN: 978-1-64746-822-4 (hardback)
ISBN: 978-1-64746-823-1 (ebook)

Available in paperback, hardback, and e-book.
Coming soon in audiobook

Any Internet addresses (websites, blogs, etc.) and telephone numbers printed in this book are offered as a resource. They are not intended in any way to be or imply an endorsement by Author Academy Elite, nor does Author Academy Elite vouch for the content of these sites and numbers for the life of this book.

Some names and identifying details have been changed to protect the privacy of individuals.

Dedication:

My darling daughter, when you were only a couple of days old, I wrote a promise in your baby book. The oath still holds true and will forever.

I hope you always know how much I love you. I will always be there for you. My heart is full of pride each and every time I think of you, and it always will be No Matter What.

Love Mom

Contents

Foreword

Monika Polefka-Proulx stresses the importance: "Follow your gut." Time and again, I've found myself repeating this sound bit of wisdom. Instinct is immeasurably powerful.

Monika's perspective in "Note to the reader" is highly relatable, with some aspects mirroring my own journey of awareness and growth.

That's not surprising, I suppose, since we have been friends for over a quarter of a century! I believe we naturally remain close to those who share similar memories, concerns, and values on our unique paths.

I smiled at the following passage written by Monika because it easily could be attributed to me—and I suspect many of us—which also speaks to the global message this book shares about the complexities of parenting and unconditional love:

"I am headstrong, stubborn, and emotional. My main weakness is still my desire to fix my children's problems, but I'm working on it, and every day I get a little bit better at butting out."

It is ironic how frequently parents-to-be worry whether they will have enough love to share because, in hindsight, it's actually letting our children fly—and fall—on their own that is more challenging.

There are comedic moments intertwined amongst very difficult, raw, and traumatic situational events. This is a story of love and helplessness that makes the novel both endearing and captivating.

There are wonderful lessons—gifts—within passages that readers can take from Monika and her family's circumstances regarding how we interpret others' opinions while staying true to ourselves.

"*Be nice* was deeply ingrained in me."—Monika

I believe this is true for many of us—any variance leading to profound questioning of ourselves and deep guilt.

Confidence may come readily to some, while others struggle a lifetime to develop the fortitude to advocate for one's self and firmly say, "enough!"

The book speaks to diversity, even amongst our families. We assume we have everything down-pat, only to discover a crinkle in our thought process since life is ever-changing, presenting new challenges despite how prepared we imagined ourselves to be! Parenthood is as much a balance of learning as it is teaching.

Readers will find themselves eagerly anticipating the next events in the novel and becoming emotionally attached, cheering successes while holding one's breath through challenges faced.

The message I took from Monika's revelations revolves around kindness and self-awareness. We each deserve gentleness, particularly when we harbour guilt about circumstances and limitations beyond our control.

Being "nice" is not a proper reaction to being victimized. We fight for those we hold dear. We need to forgive ourselves even if outsiders do not understand. After all, we are frequently our own worst critics. That has certainly been a theme in my life.

It is funny that we often find our voice when we speak on behalf of others. While bashfulness and fear are hefty deterrents in communicating, love is a powerful outlet that tends to outweigh our doubts.

When it comes to our loved ones, nothing is more important than their well-being. We find our pent-up voices are surprisingly strong, with much to convey if threatened.

"Experts know best." Except when they do not. There is no replication for the bond of love between parent and child. Better awareness of this truth has been an ongoing lesson for me, it is one that came at great personal expense and loss. Respect for authority and titles ought not to be automatic. We must earn trust.

When asked to write the foreword for Monika's book, I was deeply moved. I am grateful and honoured that Monika values my perspective and entrusted me with intimate details. This gives me pause to set in motion a long-considered endeavour, to publish my own experiences.

We all want to know we are not alone. And we need to hear stories to foster resiliency and healing and to create positive changes.

Thank you, Monika, my kind friend, for generously, candidly, and bravely sharing your family's emotional journey of love and hope.

#NoMoreSilence
Velvet Martin
*Samantha's Law

Acknowledgments

Much gratitude to the following people:

My mom, a gutsy woman, who put her children's well-being above her own needs when deciding to return to Canada. She taught me the meaning of bravery. Her resilience and self-sacrifice ultimately allowed me to write this book.

My darling husband, Mike Proulx, when all else fails, I know you always have my back through thick and thin.

My son, Karl Proulx, your support and encouragement while writing this book kept me pushing forward.

Lucy Pelletier Tomlinson and Jennifer Montpetit-Ferguson, you two ladies have been my rock for as long as I can remember. When I first took on this project, your encouragement was one of the reasons I didn't give up. You cannot imagine how much it means that both of you were as excited about this book as I was. Thank you for believing in me.

Darlene Fenske, thank you for your thoughts, encouragement, and feedback. I truly appreciate the amount of time you dedicated to helping me. You've been my sounding board, my confidant, and my friend.

Sheila Scharmann, you taught me to love the written word. Thanks for your support and comments. I hope I've made you proud.

Nicki Phillips Martin, your observations provided clarity and confidence.

My dear friend, Lorie Moir Gurnett, thanks for your prayers and support. You are a bright light that shines God's joy.

Velvet Martin, your dauntless courage is an inspiration. I am proud to call you my friend.

My editor, thank you for working closely with me and strengthening my voice.

Finally, to my amazing daughter, Samantha Cheston. Your strength, encouragement, and determination are true inspirations. Without your backing, this book would never come to be. Your mama loves you, peanut girl!

Note To The Reader

You might think to yourself, *Why should I read this book?* How can Monika understand what I'm going through or know anything about me or my child? And you are partially right; your experiences are different than mine; your child is unique. However, when I was fighting for my daughter's life, I felt utterly alone. I was desperate for solutions and ashamed about needing them, so I understand some of the pain you might be feeling.

Or perhaps your thinking, *This could never happen to me.* If so, I pray you're right! I pray your child is safe and happy, but I encourage you to read this book anyway. Hopefully, it can provide some insight into some of the problems kids face today.

I am not an expert, but I am a mom who loves her children, and I have a gift, something that until recently I thought of as a burden, a curse, destined to stifle my joy. Some people refer to it as intuition, being overly sensitive, philosophical, or emotional. Recently, the word empath has become all the rage. I've heard them all.

As I was growing up, I never truly understood why I felt such depths of emotions. I often wondered what was wrong with me. Other people seemed able to let things go while I spent my time over-analyzing everything and feeling incredible pain about events or situations far beyond my control. Watching the news was excruciating! Sitting across from someone and feeling a person's anger, happiness, or sorrow was disconcerting. Again and again, I internalized other people's emotions, confusing them for my own. So, I spent a great deal of time trying to please others. I wanted to fix things and not hurt other people's feelings. This caused me to often disregard my inner dialogue. I didn't trust my instincts and criticized myself for being overly sensitive whenever something or someone's intentions didn't feel right. More often than naught, I'd chastise myself for being foolish and ending up in a dangerous situation. Thankfully, I'm now a different person. I've learned to tune out some of the negative energies around me while also accepting and listening to my instincts. They've never steered me wrong!

I'm the result of an odd union of two people from entirely different parts of the world. My mother was born in Mexico but immigrated to Canada when she married my German father. She is beautiful, funny, easy to anger, and quick to laugh. She has struggled with mental illness for the majority of her life. It's my belief that, most likely, others in my genealogy have as well. Whether my mom's mental anguish was brought on by generational abuse, heredity, or by a similar affliction of intuitive energy is debatable.

As a child, my family spent four years living in Mexico City with my grandma, *Abuelita*. She exemplified compassion, empathy, and beauty to me; she taught me to love God. Although this book is not about religious beliefs, I feel it's necessary to discuss as it's part of who I am and, in turn, who my children are. *Abuela* was a Jehovah's Witness; yes, I'm aware that for many, the first thought is *That's a cult*. I don't know if it's a cult or not because I was a child, but I know that my *abuela* was gentle and kind.

I've heard many stories about *Abuelita's* extreme moods and intense discipline methods, but I never knew that side of her. She was always patient and loving with me. *Abuelita* was my protector; she taught me to be compassionate, and I loved her deeply. She often interjected on my behalf when my mother was punishing me, even when her interference caused friction between my mom and her. Often, she'd hug me after an especially harsh spanking.

I spent a lot of time with *Abuelita* at the kingdom hall in Mexico City. We sat together for bible studies, and I walked alongside her for weekly evangelical visits. I have a vivid memory of sitting in the tiny kitchen of a woman whose hands and feet were gnarled and contorted. My *abuelita's* faith was palpable as she held the suffering woman's hand and prayed for God's mercy.

Sitting beside my *abuela*, I first experienced the wonder of Charlton Hesston in *The Ten Commandments*, Orson Wells in *David and Goliath*, and Victor Mature in *Samson and Delilah*. I didn't understand anything about religion or God. Still, I grew up never doubting His existence. After all, *Abuelita* said he was real, so it must be so.

She taught me to wash the floors with Pine-Sol®, to get down on my knees nightly and say the Lord's Prayer, follow God's commandments, and above all, try to be a decent person. She instructed me to give to the poor (although we had nothing to share) and treat others the way I wanted to be treated. She valued truth, and in turn, taught me to do the same.

My father passed away when I was eleven years old, which prompted my mother to make the difficult decision to return to Canada and raise my sister and me in our birthplace. She was a brave woman, alone in a country without extended family, placing her children's future above her needs. Mom was also erratic, sometimes depressed, other times exuberant with joy, and occasionally verbally and physically abusive. It wasn't intentional, nor was it her fault. Her childhood had been difficult. Generational abuse is hard to break. We learn what we live.

After Daddy died and we moved back to Canada, I didn't see *Abuelita* again for many years. When I finally did, I was an adult, and she was ill and didn't know me, but I remembered her. I remembered her laughter, her mannerisms, and her faith. Her teachings stuck with me.

The northern Alberta community we moved into was small, with only one school. It was a catholic school, so morning prayers and occasional mandatory masses were involved, but other than that, we didn't go to church. My *abuelas* biblical teachings had come to an abrupt end. My mother didn't believe in organized religion. She said faith was private, and she didn't see the need to belong to a congregation. In truth, I think she was angry with God. Regardless of our lack of fellowship, I never questioned God's existence. I guess I figured it was better to be safe than sorry.

As I grew, I continued to recite the Lord's prayer at night, and I occasionally found myself bartering with God for one thing or another. I thought that's how it worked! Everyday mundane trades were part of my belief system.

"Dear God, please don't let my mom give my puppy away. I promise I'll help her more. Dear God, please don't let my mom find out I was smoking. If she doesn't find out, I'll try to be nicer to my sister."

With that, I went along my merry way, merely hoping for the best but secretly expecting the worst. Why should good things happen to me when so many bad things were happening in the world? It was my subconscious belief that I was destined to experience loss, and my family was cursed. We didn't have money. Most of the women ended up widowed. We weren't highly educated, and loss was part of everyday life. So, I was certain I would end up like my mother and grandmother—alone.

I was just a teenager when I started dating my future husband, Mike. At the time, religion was unimportant to me. Mike was agnostic, and although I thought God existed, I didn't feel the need to go to church. I had adopted my mom's philosophy. For the most part, I hoped God would forgive my mistakes and help me through the rough patches, but I didn't really expect Him to. As long as I did my best, I supposed I'd manage. Every painful experience was measured against losing my father—my hero. It was my compass; I used it to tell myself I could survive anything after having survived his death. Little did I know, pain can't be placed into neat compartments, and there is nothing like the heartache a parent feels for their child.

I'm not a perfect mother, far from it! I have tried to emulate *Abuela's* teachings of right and wrong, but I've made millions of mistakes along the way. I was sometimes overly permissive, and other times exceptionally harsh. I've said and done things I'm not proud of. I have moments and events I wish I could change and other memories that, to this day, bring a smile to my face. I am headstrong, stubborn, and emotional. My main weakness is still my desire to fix my children's problems, but I'm working on it, and every day I get a little bit better at butting out.

Raising children often felt like an uphill battle. Still, Mike and I have fought long and hard to provide an environment of unconditional love. We've tried to teach our kids right from wrong, and our reward has been incredibly close relationships with both of them. Nonetheless, my daughter Samantha and I occasionally butt heads. Daughters and mothers often clash. It's complicated the same way it was for *Abuela* and Mom.

As you read this book, I expect there will be times you will wonder what the heck I was thinking and other times, you may be able to relate to the struggles. When our family was living our own personal hell, I felt utterly and completely alone, so I hope that sharing our story will reach out and touch others who may be feeling equally abandoned.

I truly believe that some of the most painful things we endure in life are meant to make us grow and become better human beings. If everything was easy, we would never change; we would become stagnant and lose our ability to feel real joy. The journey is both excruciating and rewarding beyond belief.

CHAPTER 1

Gone

She was gone again! We had to find her! The last time it took two weeks to locate her, two weeks of fear, anger, and worry. But this time was far worse. I could feel it in my bones. Something terrible was going to happen. My mind kept drifting back to all of the Facebook messages I'd read that day, each memory invoking further panic. *What if we can't find her? We have to get to her fast, but I've already been searching for hours. Don't panic; breathe. Keep it together!*

My cellphone rang; it was Mike. He wasn't having any luck either. He wanted to meet up and keep searching together.

"I don't know; I think we should search separately. That way, we can cover more ground."

The tightness in my chest was becoming unbearable. I could feel my composure slipping. The desire to give in to fear and break down was rising to my throat. Quickly I pushed it down and instinctively reached under my front seat. My hand brushed against the cold steel. *It's still there, good.*

1

"Okay, let's meet in an hour if we haven't found her," I shakily answered. My voice cracked a little, but I shook my head— *no time to cry.*

CHAPTER 2

Beautiful Gift, Beautiful Life

Could I be pregnant? No! Maybe? For two weeks, the thought randomly popped into my mind. It was most likely a wishful thought, but nonetheless, I snuck away to the local drugstore and bought a home pregnancy test while my husband Mike bathed our two-year-old son and got him ready for bed. Upon returning, I tiptoed into our on-suite to urinate on the little white stick.

"Monika? Can you get Karl a snack while I put him in his PJs?" Mike hollered.

"In a minute. I'm in the bathroom!"

How long does this take? I wondered while pacing back and forth, anxiously awaiting the results. Slowly, a faint line began to appear. Widening my eyes, I leaned forward and stared as the forming lines flickered from a light shadow to a solid plus sign. Surprised, I picked up the stick and carefully examined it. *Don't get excited yet! This can't be right! Maybe it's faulty?*

The idea we could get pregnant without prior planning had never crossed my mind. I had assumed it wasn't possible for us. With Karl, we'd spent a year of hormone treatments. I'd had monthly physical exams, daily temperature readings, and the occasional random midday phone call to Mike when my temperature was right! Prior to finding myself making these phone calls, I'd always assumed people didn't really do that!

How could I suddenly be pregnant? We hadn't even been trying! I was shocked, a little uneasy, and afraid of getting too excited. We had been discussing the idea, but I'd been hesitating. The previous year I'd miscarried and been heartbroken by the loss. It was a trying time. Conceiving had proven to be as difficult as the first time, and we'd lost the baby on the very day we'd decided to share our good news. I'd slumped into a state of anxiety and self-reproach, blaming myself for the loss because, against Mike's wishes, I'd shovelled snow the previous day.

After Mike put Karl to bed, I nervously showed him the pregnancy test and said, "Does this look like a plus sign to you?" Wide-eyed, Mike nodded and grinned.

"Are you sure?" he asked.

"No . . . not really!"

The next morning, I headed back to the drugstore and purchased two more tests, which again were positive. Still unable to believe our good fortune, I followed up by making a doctor's appointment for final confirmation.

After the doctor's appointment, I immediately became convinced we were having a girl. Instinctually, I gravitated towards pink items. I purchased a pink housecoat with matching pink slippers while referring to the baby as "she." I browsed through little girl's clothing and fantasized about little dresses, tiny fancy shoes, and endless hours of brushing long hair. When expecting our son, Karl, it'd been the exact same way.

Although I had always imagined myself with a little girl, I'd immediately known I was carrying a boy.

A few months after our surprise pregnancy, we went to visit Mike's grandparents. Mike's grandfather asked if he could predict the baby's gender.

"Sure, but I'm having a girl," I cheekily replied as I laid out on the living room couch.

Grandpa threaded a needle and hung it above my belly like a pendulum. Folklore states if the needle swings back and forth, you're having a boy, but if it turns in a circle, you're having a girl. In our case, the needle forcefully swung back and forth, and Mike's grandpa gleefully announced, "You're definitely having another boy."

I, however, shook my head. "Nope, I know I'm having a girl," I responded confidently.

"We'll see," he answered.

Right from the beginning, this pregnancy was different. In my mind, the contrasts further confirmed my conviction. I was having a daughter. While carrying Karl, I'd experienced three months of horrible morning sickness, followed by six months of ravenous appetite. Once I'd ate six pork chops in one sitting! Not only was I always hungry, but I'd also remained incredibly busy. I'd worked full-time up to two weeks before Karl's birth and had been actively involved with the upgrades to our new home. I refused to sit still, which had lead to torn abdomen muscles on my right side from sprinting up and down the stairs with buckets full of water. But with this pregnancy, I often felt weak and lightheaded. I experienced shortness of breath and lacked appetite. Gaining weight proved to be quite difficult. So, upon my doctor's orders, I'd started supplementing my meals with Boost® and forcing food down my throat. Every pound gained was a victory.

This baby sat much higher than Karl. Karl had laid low in my abdomen, heavily leaning on my pelvis, but this new baby was squishing my ribs, taking my breath away. I was always pushing on my stomach, trying to guide her down. In addition, I became increasingly anxious with fear of losing consciousness. Once while in the shower, I fainted. Another time while grocery shopping with Karl, I'd nearly lost consciousness. I had to stop, lean heavily against the cart, and focus on taking deep breaths until the room spun back into focus. It was unnerving. I didn't want to hurt myself or the baby, and I certainly didn't want to scare Karl. So I stayed close to home.

My increasing anxiety and moody disposition led me to seek out a counsellor. I was still feeling guilty about the previous miscarriage, and because I was struggling to gain weight while dealing with vertigo, I feared another. My emotions were erratic. I cried at the drop of a hat, flashbacks of past traumas popped in my head at inopportune times, and old resentments towards my mother caused friction between us. I spent many a session discussing my anger about past hurts or expressing my overwhelming fear that something would go wrong with the baby.

On April 30th, I woke to light cramping, which continued throughout the day. Just like Karl, the contractions started six days before the due date. We had plans to take part in our small town's annual car rally. The car rally consisted of various checkpoints throughout the community. The object of the game was to be the first car full to complete all the tasks. After which, there would be a barbeque and dance. I was supposed to be the designated driver for our group. But although my cramping was slight, we lived forty-five minutes away from the hospital, and I wasn't keen on delivering with a car full of most likely intoxicated people. So I cancelled our sitter, and we stayed home. At around 5:00 p.m., the contractions intensified and began coming consistently every four minutes.

Because I'd been told second births progress quicker, we left Karl with his aunt and headed to the hospital.

"My wife is in labour!" Mike excitedly announced to the receptionist. She knowingly smirked and told us to take a seat. When the next contraction hit, it doubled me over, and I nearly lost my balance, at which point she quickly checked us in and ushered us to obstetrics. Upon examination, the nurse said, "You're three centimetres dilated."

So we settled in for what was expected to be a long night. The intensity of each contraction increased at a steady pace. A nurse asked if I wanted something for the pain, and I declined. With Karl, I'd felt every contraction in my back, so the staff gave me two morphine shots, which had made me throw up profusely, but this labour was in my abdomen, and I desperately wanted to try for a completely natural birth.

As each spasm racked through my body, Mike stroked my hair and encouraged me. "You're doing great, babe. Breathe, you're doing great."

I listened to him count backwards and willed myself to relax as the contractions steadily increased in frequency and strength. It felt like I was being torn apart from the inside out; I could barely catch my breath between each shooting pain. When one subsided, I hollered at a nurse that I'd changed my mind and wanted something but was quickly informed it was too late.

"I don't think I can make it," I croaked. My throat was dry, I was thirsty, and the little ice chips were of no use. I wanted water! At this point, Mike's face turned chalk-white, and he stumbled backwards and staggered towards a chair. *What's his problem?* I thought before another body-wrenching contraction took over my senses, but I was no longer on anyone's radar. The nurses had utterly changed their focus!

Three nurses hovered around Mike and began rushing back and forth with wet cloths, crackers, and water. One nurse was gently patting his back, a second was encouraging him to take a drink, while the third helped him sit down. It was ridiculous. I wondered if I was watching a poorly made cartoon or if someone was going to jump out from behind a curtain and say, "*You're on candid camera.*"

As the next contraction ripped through my abdomen, no one noticed. I willed myself through it while the nurses continued to hover around their new patient. Once it subsided, I breathlessly said, "Hello, I'm having a baby here!" One of the nurses looked up at me in astonishment then took a step away from Mike. "Yes, I'm still here," I sarcastically said as she rushed in my direction.

Labour progressed rather quickly from that point onward. Earlier, the doctor had stopped in to examine me; she'd assured me she'd be keeping her pager with her all night, but now they were having difficulty reaching her. After several attempts, they tried to contact another physician. "Where is my doctor? When will she be here?" I breathlessly demanded.

"I'm sorry, we haven't been able to reach her, and the other doctor is too far away to arrive in time, but don't worry, we know what we're doing," a nurse responded.

"No . . . I want my doctor," I shrieked in panic. At least with Karl, a resident doctor had been on duty. But without a doctor available, my hysteria was taking over. "I need a doctor in case something goes wrong! I want a doctor!"

Mike was once more standing by my side, although he seemed rather unsteady. His eyes were slightly glazed, and his hand felt clammy against mine. *I sure hope he keeps it together,* I thought.

An overwhelming pressure gripped my abdomen. Baby wanted out! "I want to push," I screamed, but the nurses shook their heads and urged me to hold on.

"The doctor is on her way! She'll be here any minute."

The need to bear down intensified; I didn't think I could hold off, and then when I could no longer stand the pressure, the urge passed.

It was at this point that the doctor rushed in and said, "Okay, Monika, how are you doing? You can go ahead and give us a big push."

I recall a split second where I thought, *I don't feel the urge,* but I bared down nonetheless, and fire ripped through my pelvis. Hysterically I tried to push myself up and leap off the bed. The intense burning between my legs had sent me into a frenzy. *Something was wrong! What was that? I'm not doing this!*

"I don't want to do this," I cried, shaking my head back and forth.

"You have to. It's okay. You can do this," Mike kept repeating while preventing me from getting up.

"I can't . . . it hurts, I can't do this. I don't want to . . . please." I sobbed.

At precisely 8:50 p.m., weighing six pounds three ounces and eighteen inches in length, my beautiful peanut girl, Samantha Michelle Proulx, was born. I reached to hold her, but they quickly whisked her away to an examining table at the end of the room. Helplessly I watched them vigorously rub her little body. It seemed she wasn't responding as expected! My mind jumped to horrible scenarios. I choked out, "How is she?" In my frightened state, I was sure they were avoiding my questions. They appeared to be speaking rapidly, and she wasn't crying.

I remember asking over and over again, "Is she okay? Is she okay?" Time stood still. *Is she okay? Please give me my baby. Why is she not crying? Why are you hovering around her? What's wrong with her?* Finally, they swaddled her in a tiny pink blanket and gently placed her in my arms. I looked down at her beautiful little face, and bright blue eyes stared back at me.

"She's perfect," I whispered. Cautiously, I opened the blanket and counted her ten tiny toes and fingers. Her head was completely bald, her skin equally smooth, and her button nose was precisely like her dad's. "She has your nose," I whispered, looking lovingly at Mike. Silently I thanked God. I had carried this baby girl in my womb for nine months while battling severe anxiety about her birth. *What if something went wrong? What if she was sick? What if I miscarried again? What if I didn't have enough love in me for another child? What if . . . what if?* Scenario upon scenario had tortured my every waking moment, but she was here, and my heart was full.

As I held Samantha in my arms, the doctor started the daunting task of stitching me. The sheering pain I'd experienced during my first push was a large tare. Afterwards, a nurse took Samantha, and with Mike in tow, left the room. A second nurse tried to clean me up, but I insisted on taking a shower, so she gingerly helped me stand. With fake bravado, I assured her I was fine, then proceeded to take two unsteady steps forward, followed by a near tumble. I was exhausted and weak from blood loss.

Mike returned, holding Sam close to his chest; she was tightly swaddled, freshly clean, and wearing a knitted pink hat. The nurse followed him in and asked if I needed help getting her to latch.

"I'm not planning on nursing," I responded.

Disapprovingly, the nurse tossed her head and said, "Are you sure? It's better for the baby."

"Yes, I'm sure. I want to bottle feed her," I hesitantly explained.

I had nursed Karl for the first two months of his life, but I'd had problems producing enough milk. It had been terribly stressful not providing enough, so I didn't want to do it again.

"Tsk . . . tsk . . . okay, I'll go get a bottle." She relented. I felt chastised but sure of my choice. When she returned, she handed the bottle to Mike and abruptly marched out of the room. Sleepily, I drifted off while Mike fed Samantha. A few hours later, I awoke to a dark room, and the steady sound of monitors filled the silence. Mike had gone home for the night, the baby had been taken to the nurses' station, and I was alone. Gingerly, I turned on my side and drifted off to asleep.

The following morning upon waking, I asked for my baby. Smiling, the morning nurse brought her to me and said, "She slept like an angel, only waking up once at five a.m. for a feeding. We let you sleep because you needed your rest. Now, let's get you prepped for nursing."

"I'm going to be bottle feeding her," I responded. Narrowing her eyes, she critically replied, "Oh . . . you know, nursing is the best option for the baby."

I stammered, "I know . . . but, ugh . . . I've decided not to nurse."

Samantha and I stayed in the hospital one more night. It was long enough; I couldn't wait to get out of there and back to my little boy, Karl. Plus, every single time they handed me a bottle, I felt reproached. Even upon discharge, they told me the benefits of breast milk over formula. *Was I a bad mother for not wanting to nurse?* "I'm not going to breastfeed," I haltingly replied.

"Okay . . . if you're certain, take this; it will stop your milk production," the nurse grudgingly replied. Feeling somewhat ashamed, I took two small pills in my right hand and chased them down with a gulp of cold water.

At home, Sam continued to sleep for long stretches. She ate every four hours during the day but only woke once at night. It was crazy! *How often does a baby sleep until four or five in the morning since day one?* I could hardly believe my good fortune. *I'd hit the jackpot and birthed the most amazing baby in the world!* Her ease was a much-needed reprieve because I wasn't bouncing back as quickly as I had with Karl. I was exhausted; the dark circles under my eyes seemed to be getting darker. I felt weak, anxious, and sad, plus I was also producing large amounts of milk unexpectedly.

Two days after getting home, I found myself painfully engorged with beet red melons for breasts. They were hard as rocks, radiating heat across my torso. *How could this be? I was supposed to be drying up, not overproducing!*

In desperation, I called my doctors' office and asked if I should nurse Samantha. "Absolutely not; it's too late," the nurse responded. Crying, I requested something for the pain.

"Put warm compresses on your breasts, take warm showers, and it will pass in a couple of days. This is a common side effect of the pill." Defeated and feeling chastised, I wondered why they hadn't told me the side effects before.

The next few days were dreadful. Every movement was excruciating. It was hard to lift my arms, which was problematic with a newborn and a toddler.

Samantha was a joyful baby. She was always happy, smiling, and cooing. I used to say that if all babies were as easy as Sam, I would have five more. She loved to sit in her swing, watch the dog run around the house, or bounce in her jolly jumper. Her chubby legs were always kicking.

Karl was her favourite person in the world. Her eyes lit up every time he looked at her. He was the first to get her to laugh. And she giggled happily at everything he did. He was always entertaining her with silly faces, peek-a-boo, or by kissing her chubby hands. Their mutual love was adorable.

As a baby, Karl had been the complete opposite of Sam. My poor boy had been awfully colicky—there were days upon days where he screamed for hours, his little legs scrunched up in pain. Sometimes, Mike would come home from work; I'd meet him at the door, hand him our screaming son and walk out in tears. Sam was different; everything seemed easy with her. Even when she was sick, she was a joy. She'd smile through her stomach aches and runny noses. Everyone seemed to love her. Wherever we went, complete strangers stopped to stare. Sam's sweet cherubic face, fair skin, blue eyes, and blond hair, and Karl's completely opposite dark complexion, dark brown hair, and eyes made them a striking pair.

I was young when I had my first child, Karl. As a first-time mom of twenty-two years, I was overly sensitive to other people's opinions. Comments or criticism from older generations often led me to question my parenting skills. *How does one learn to parent, if not by example? Parenting skills are not taught in schools. I wish they were.*

Being a good parent was incredibly important to me. I was going to do things differently. *My children would never be spanked, and words of encouragement would always come from my mouth.* Or so I thought! Most parents have similar expectations. But when I felt criticized for *spoiling* Karl by rocking him to sleep and allowing him to come to our room, I followed the advice given, and Mike and I worked on making Karl stay in his own bed. It led to months of nightly crying episodes, which were awful for Karl and made me feel ashamed. So, I was determined to not make the same "mistake" and overindulge Samantha. She learned to self-soothe at a very young age. Fortunately, she was a breeze to put to bed; she hardly ever cried and almost always fell asleep without much fuss. In retrospect, I regret not *spoiling* her a little more as a newborn, but I was impressionable and far too worried about other people's opinions. Now that I'm older and a grandmother, I know better! Time goes by too quickly, you can't spoil a baby, and there is no such thing as too much love!

In the mornings, Karl and I would wake Sam by singing to her. "Sammy dooby, Sammy Sammy dooby. Poopy doopy, Poopy Poopy dooby." It was a silly made-up song inspired by her grandfather, who nicknamed her Sammy Doo, even though we wanted to call her Samantha or Sam. I thought Sammy sounded like a dog's name! But the name stuck, and soon enough, we composed the Sammy doo song! She loved it; she'd pull herself up against her crib railing and bounce happily to the words.

At the age of nine months, Sammy started crawling. Shortly after her first birthday, she began to walk, which quickly turned into running. She adored Karl and emulated his every move. The two of them would spend hours playing with toy cars, rolling balls around the house, and wrestling imaginary bad guys. Baby dolls were of no interest to her.

When Sam turned two, she began to assert herself. It was like a switch went off. She went from my happy, loving baby to an independent, headstrong toddler. She was extraordinarily inquisitive and was always reaching to touch one forbidden object after another. A simple "no" had always worked with Karl, but Sammy was a different story. She would look at us, purse her little lips, and do it again. Tapping her fingers wasn't a deterrent; her bottom lip would quiver, her eyes would swell with tears, she'd place the two middle fingers from her right hand in her mouth for comfort, then she'd reach out and grab it again. It didn't matter how many times we told her no. Once she decided she wanted something, she wouldn't give up. Her determination was both frustrating and admirable at the same time. In defeat, we completely toddler-proofed the house; we removed every breakable item from reach, a task we'd never found necessary before.

Our nightly bedtime routine included storytime. I've always cherished books, so I tried to instill that in my children. Karl loved storytime, but Sammy was easily distracted. She liked looking at the pictures in the books but would promptly lose interest in the stories. I tried to capture her curiosity, but she was easily bored.

On the other hand, colouring was one of her favourite activities. She'd sit down and quietly colour for hours. Unfortunately, she had a tendency to write on everything. Furniture, walls, clothing, and books were all fair game. It was a regular occurrence. From experience, I know that permanent markers can't be removed from cloth furniture, and the Magic Eraser® is excellent at cleaning crayon-streaked walls.

To socialize the children, I started taking them to weekly "Mommy and Me" playgroups. Through the group, I formed a lasting friendship with another mom, Diana. Her children and mine were close in age. We started having regular play-dates. While the kids ran around, we'd share our hopes and dreams for their futures. I recall many conversations about our girls. They both had a lot of spunk and often ended up fighting over a toy or what game they wanted to play. Diana and I would jokingly say they would end up one of two ways: Strong independent women no one would dare push around, or if we weren't careful, bullies.

One evening when Sam was two and a half, I put the children to bed, kissed them good night, and went to the basement to watch television with Mike. About an hour later, we heard movement upstairs, followed by a woman's voice. Startled, Mike and I rushed upstairs and discovered Mrs. Cade standing in our kitchen, holding Samantha. *She lived two blocks away, so why was she in our kitchen with our daughter!* Sasha, our bichon puppy, was running around her legs barking excitedly. Taken aback, I reached for Sammy and asked, "Can I help you?"

"Does she belong to you?"

I was confused— *of course, she belongs to me; you're in my kitchen holding her,* I reasoned. "Yes, she's our daughter," I replied.

"I saw her running by my house, chasing this little dog, so I picked her up and followed the puppy. Fortunately, it led me here."

"I don't understand," I stammered.

I'd put the children to bed; both had been asleep when I went downstairs, *so how did Sam get out of the house without our knowledge!*

All of our doors were equipped with swing guards because Karl had horrific nightmares and often sleepwalked. We were afraid he would leave the house during the night, so we had installed extra security.

That evening, Sammy woke up, pulled a chair over and opened the door to let Sasha out. Sasha bolted, and Sammy followed after her. Thankfully, Mrs. Cade had spotted her! Even now, years later, I shiver when I think about that night. It was frightening. Sam had left the house, and we hadn't even heard her!

After that evening, I spent many months on high alert. Sam was always trying to leave the house. She loved being outdoors, which kept me on my toes at all hours. We stacked chairs nightly so that she couldn't pull them over to the doors. We replaced the swing bars with chains and installed baby-proof handles. This helped for a while, but she was incredibly resourceful and quickly learned to maneuver the childproof doorknobs!

CHAPTER 3

Colouring Outside
The Lines

My mother was widowed at a young age and raised two young daughters alone. We were in Mexico when Dad died, but Mom chose to return to Canada and bring us to our native land. She felt it was our birthright to grow up in our own country. Although she had no family in Canada, she made the sacrifice for my sister and me.

Mom struggled with depression and emotional instability throughout the majority of her life. She grew up in an impoverished household with a single mother and five other siblings. My *abuela* did her best, but she'd never had a good role model. Her childhood had been riddled with abuse and neglect, and as an adult, she'd been widowed three times. Life had not been easy.

After my dad died, I'd become convinced our family was cursed! I don't know if I overheard a conversation or simply drew my own conclusions, but I secretly assumed I'd end up alone.

When I was fourteen years old, I met Mike, and against most people's advice, we married the year I graduated from high school. We were in love, full of dreams, and determined to be together. Neither one of us had money, so Mike took out a $5,000 loan to fund our nuptials. He worked as a mechanic, and I worked part-time as a cashier while completing high school.

I had big dreams; I wanted to become a child psychologist and work with children suffering from trauma. (It stemmed from the loneliness and disconnect I'd felt as a child. I'd been extremely shy, a quiet girl who struggled with low self-esteem and often used fake bravado to deal with inner turmoil.) However, we couldn't afford higher education, so I took a job in a daycare instead.

Everyday life took over—we had Karl, and I gave up on my dream of becoming a psychologist. However, I still wanted a career. I didn't want to be dependant on Mike. My deepest fear was of finding myself alone, destitute, and unable to provide for my son. So, I started taking night classes.

I decided on accounting because although I didn't particularly like the idea of working with numbers, the school was a direct drive into north Edmonton. My lack of confidence made it impossible to consider driving too deeply into the city. Afraid I might not be able to hack it and not wanting to waste my time, I decided to enroll in the course I dreaded the most, Economics. I figured I might as well get it out of the way. Surprisingly, I ended up enjoying the program. I found the checks and balances reassuring. For the next few years, I continued taking evening classes. It was a slow, tedious process. What was a two-year program full-time was going to be five to ten years part-time.

Life was very busy. I was working two to three days a week, parenting my two small children, and taking evening courses. Mike worked long hours and rushed home to watch the children while I went to classes. Sometimes we barely saw one another.

One evening while I was in class, Karl thrashed about in his sleep with a horrific nightmare in which he begged Mike not to kill him. Karl's nightmares were becoming violent and frightening to witness.

"I couldn't calm him down; he was afraid of me," Mike whispered when I returned.

Unsure of what was causing Karl's bad dreams, we sought medical attention and were told he was experiencing night terrors.

"He's a textbook case and should outgrow them by the time he's twelve."

We were frightened. The night terrors were horrific to witness, but Karl was asleep and never remembered a thing. "Don't wake him. Just follow him around and prevent him from accidentally falling down the stairs and hurting himself." The doctor instructed.

It seemed like simple enough advice from someone not witnessing their child running around the house, shaking, convulsing and crying every night. For us, it wasn't simple. Seeing Karl terrified while trapped in the dream was heart-breaking. We wanted to fix it. So against their advice, we tried various methods to refocus his attention and break the cycle. We started giving him a glass of water and discovered that if Karl managed to focus on drinking, he'd snap out of the nightmare, instantly calm down, and go back to sleep. As an additional countermeasure, we'd wake him an hour after he'd fallen asleep. This seemed to interrupt the process.

Around this same time, Sam was throwing up daily. She'd always had a weak stomach, even as a baby. Strawberries, raspberries, pies, apples, oatmeal, and yogurt made her gag, but vomiting suddenly became such a regular occurrence she no longer bothered to tell me. Sometimes, Sammy would wake in the middle of the night, make her way to the bathroom, throw up, and wobble back to bed. I'd awaken to the sound of her gagging and go to her, but she rarely cried about it. Other times she'd wake me to tell me Karl was having a night terror, and while I was occupied with him, she'd go to the bathroom and throw up.

Once, we were eating breakfast at a local restaurant; her uncle bought each of the children a hot chocolate with whipped cream.

Sam didn't want to try it. She kept saying, "I puke." He thought she was silly and put the spoon to her mouth. The creamy white foam barely touched her lips when she started to gag and vomited on the floor.

Concerned over the frequency of her stomach problems, we took her to see the doctor. Despite medical tests, everything came back normal. They assured us there was nothing to worry about; her development was on track.

Karl had been thoroughly potty trained by two, but Sam didn't show much interest, so I didn't start training until she was nearing three, even though they say girls are so much easier than boys. Once I began, I expected it to be a breeze. It wasn't—it was a battle! She hated the potty, cried when I put her on the seat, and fought me at every turn. After months, she continued having accidents and began hiding her wet underwear behind the toilet, under her bed, or in the garbage. Several times she flushed them, and we had to get a plumber to unclog the bathroom.

Sammy also struggled with bedwetting, and since Pull-Ups® were expensive, we'd put her to bed, wait a little while, then pick her up and place her on the toilet while she still slept. We'd say, "Sammy, pee!"

Once, Mike jokingly said, "Sammy, pee," while I was still holding her in my arms, and she did. He roared!

Sammy was openly affectionate, empathetic, quick to express her love, and always smiling. If she witnessed someone in distress, her big blue eyes swelled up with tears, and heartfelt sobs wracked her little body. This was especially true when an animal was hurt. Her heart was pure, but she was also impulsive and stubborn. She didn't think through her actions. When an idea struck, she acted upon it. Once, when she was three years old, while outside playing with Karl, she impulsively picked up a small stone and used it to draw on my sister's new car. She wanted to make a "pretty picture for Aunty." My sister was furious, and Mike and I were mortified, but Sam was surprised by our reactions. She thought it looked nice!

If Sam was embarrassed or angry, she'd throw a temper tantrum. Sometimes she'd cry inconsolably while running to her bedroom and slamming her door. On other occasions, she'd shut down completely. She'd place the two middle fingers from her right hand in her mouth and silently glare, refusing to speak. It was impossible to get her to budge. Once, I was trying to make her apologize for not listening to her uncle, and she wouldn't. She pursed her lips tightly shut and shook her head. It was frustrating, and I was embarrassed. *Why wouldn't she just apologize?* I felt like a failure. I didn't want her to be seen as rude or self-centered, but I couldn't figure out how to get her to respond. Nothing I did worked.

It wasn't long before I realized family members and friends reacted differently to Sammy than Karl. He was more pliable and eager to please, and although she was sweet and loving, she was higher maintenance. She demanded constant attention, required a lot of supervision and regular encouragement. Most people were quickly annoyed and short with her. This angered me; I was protective of her, especially because I, too, was losing my patience! The guilt I often felt about my own frustration, coupled with other people's reactions to her, caused a lot of friction between family members and me.

In response, I went into a state of high alert, afraid to turn my back on her for a second. She was always trying to sneak out of the house and had taken to colouring on everything in sight. "Why do you keep doing this?" I shrieked after once again scrubbing down the playroom walls.

"I don't . . . know . . . Mommy," she stammered between sobs, but the next day she did it again. We hid pens, markers, and crayons from her, yet she always found something to use; I was at my wits end.

When Karl started school, I decided to go back to work and began searching for a reliable babysitter. After much deliberation, I settled on Mrs. Steward. Mrs. Steward was a large woman with ample bosom and a booming voice. She wore her dark hair in a tight bun at the nape of her neck and moved her arms about excitedly when speaking. Her husband had passed away unexpectedly. Having no children of her own, she'd taken to watching other people's. Mrs. Steward lived two blocks away from the school and was often seen picking up and dropping off her charges. This was important to Mike and me; we weren't comfortable with Karl walking independently.

At first, Karl and Sammy were happy. They liked Mrs. Steward and looked forward to spending time with her and the other children in her care. When I'd pick them up after work, both kids would joyfully bound out and animatedly describe their day. However, as time went on, I began noticing subtle changes.

What had started out as a home with a couple of children suddenly appeared overcrowded, loud and uncontrolled. When approaching the door, the atmosphere was often chaotic! The house was cluttered and tumultuous.

When dropping off the children, Sam was often crying, and I had to pry her out of my arms. "Don't worry, she calms right down after your gone," Mrs. Steward explained as she pulled Sammy into her arms, and I rushed away.

Many children, including Karl, often carried pictures and handmade crafts at pick-up time, which they'd proudly parade in front of their parents. Sammy, however, never had a project or a colouring sheet. A few times, I asked about Sam's picture, and Mrs. Steward always had a response. "Sam didn't want to colour, Sam was taking a nap, or Sam was busy playing."

It didn't make sense because I knew how much Sammy loved to colour. Still, I was afraid of being rude or hurting Mrs. Steward's feelings by questioning her too closely. *Be nice* was deeply ingrained in me.

More and more, when I picked up the kids, I found Sam sitting in a corner having time out. "What happened?" I'd ask.

"She had a temper tantrum, or she wet her underwear again," was a usual response.

Placing Sam in a quiet space for discipline if she was misbehaving was a tactic Mike and I used at home. However, we didn't punish her for having bathroom accidents. Still, I didn't question it, even when my instincts were starting to suspect something wasn't quite right. I hadn't yet learned to follow my intuition.

One evening, after months of nagging suspicion, I picked up the kids and Samantha had a white sock securely taped around her right hand.

"What is this?" I challenged.

"It's there to stop her from sucking her fingers."

"Why?" I replied in confusion.

Immediately, Mrs. Steward appeared surprised by my reaction. "She needs to stop sucking on those fingers," she confidently retorted.

I was indignant and upset, but I was *nice*, so I swallowed my anger and calmly said, "I would prefer it if you didn't put a sock on Sam's hand." Why I didn't say what was truly on my mind baffles me. *Never wrap a sock around her hand again!*

I discussed the event with Mike, and together we decided to start looking for a new sitter. However, I still wanted to be amiable. So while I started putting feelers out, I wasn't overly ambitious. *After all, what if I was simply overreacting, being paranoid, overly sensitive, or too protective!*

Time went on, and although I regularly asked Karl and Sammy if they were happy at Mrs. Stewards, I didn't get any definitively negative responses from either of them. Sammy's vocabulary was limited, so I spent extra time questioning Karl. "Promise me you'll tell me if you don't like it there, okay?"

"Yes, Mom."

At home, Samantha was increasingly difficult. She was constantly acting out. Potty training was still a battle, and her need for nonstop attention was exhausting. When in trouble, she'd sometimes bawl, "I'm a bad girl." Her words troubled me because we made a point of never telling the kids they were bad. Instead, we focused on using vocabulary that expressed our displeasure with bad behaviour, but never *with them*, and still, I didn't put it together. My problem with setting clear boundaries was placing my children in danger.

One evening, I picked up the kids, and Samantha ran into my arms sobbing. I asked what was going on, and Mrs. Steward said Sam was throwing another tantrum. Placing Sammy down, I wiped her snotty nose and cleaned the tears from her cheeks. She'd obviously been crying for quite some time. Her breath came in ragged little stutters.

I glared at Mrs. Steward. Her face was stoic, and my chest tightened with immense anger. Quickly, I packed up the kids and left.

"See you tomorrow," she snapped and closed the door.

Once home, Sammy calmed down. We ate supper, and I asked the kids what had happened. Neither one of them said much, but I was certain something was wrong.

That evening after Samantha was in bed, I sat with Karl and read him a bedtime story, after which I again questioned him about their day.

At first, he wouldn't say much, but eventually, he whispered, "Sammy got into trouble for not eating her lunch."

"Why? What was for lunch?"

With a deep swallow, he hesitantly replied, "Cherry pie."

"No, not dessert silly, what was for lunch?"

"Umm . . . nothing, we had cherry pie, and Sammy wouldn't eat it."

Samantha didn't eat cherries. She actually didn't eat most red things. Strawberries, cherries, and jams made her vomit. They had since she was a baby.

"So, what did Sammy have for lunch?" I questioned.

"She had to stay at the table until she ate all her pie."

Distressed, Samantha had eventually forced herself to eat the pie, after which she'd promptly thrown up and been placed in a corner as punishment. When Sammy had begun to suck on her fingers for comfort, Mrs. Steward had taped a sock around her hand. Sam had spent the rest of the day in the corner.

Taking a deep breath, I placed a fake smile on my face and asked, "Has Sammy been punished like this before?"

"Sometimes," he replied.

"Why?" I asked.

"She doesn't listen or do nice things. Mrs. Steward gets mad, so she can't make pictures."

"What do you mean?'

"Mrs. Steward says she can't colour if she can't do it nice."

I was enraged with Mrs. Steward and with myself! *How could I have been so stupid?* Why hadn't I listened to my gut? Suddenly, her morning tears, the acting out, and saying she was a bad girl all made sense, and I felt sick at the thought.

After kissing Karl goodnight and reassuring him it was okay to tell me what was happening, I angrily paced and ranted at Mike. "What are we going to do? The kids can't go back there!"

They never went back. My mom watched them until I was able to find a permanent caregiver, but I didn't confront Mrs. Steward, either, although I was furious. Instead, I told her the kids would be spending the summer with my mom. Even with how mad I was, I didn't want to hurt her feelings. I still wanted to be *nice*.

CHAPTER 4

Unravelling

Sam's love of music was apparent from a very young age. She was always singing and dancing around the house, so when she turned four and was *finally* fully potty trained, we enrolled her in dance classes. Initially, she refused to let me out of her sight, but once she joined in, she was enthralled.

Shania Twain was one of her favourite singers. Sam spent hours watching Shania on CMT, copying her every movement. She was really good for a four-year-old! A few times, I was taken aback by her ability to perform dance moves I thought were too suggestive for a child. Even so, I loved watching the pure joy on her face as she twirled around the house, ecstatic with the freedom of movement. She was so expressive and uninhibited.

Sam was an active child; when not singing and dancing around the house, she was busy digging in the sandbox, riding her tricycle, or playing with our dog, Sasha. Sammy loved playing with her but desperately wanted a kitten. Her first word was "cat," and her favourite toy was a flattened stuffed tabby cat that looked like roadkill. She carried that thing everywhere. She wouldn't sleep without it and cried whenever I had to wash it.

I knew eventually we'd have to give in and get her a kitten, but Mike was adamant he didn't want one. His mom was allergic, and he'd never particularly liked cats. He was a dog person.

"You won't be able to hold out forever," I'd laughingly say. "She's destined to own one!"

Our neighbours had teenage daughters that often babysat for us, so when their feline gave birth, they asked if Sammy would like to see the kittens. From that day forward, all Samantha wanted to do was visit the kitties. Getting her to come home was a battle. In true Samantha form, if she wasn't asking to call on the neighbours, she began trying to sneak out and go there. Every day she begged us to let her get a kitty.

After weeks of nagging, she wore Mike down, and he took her next door to choose one. When they came back, she was happily holding a scraggly-looking calico.

"Are you sure you want that one?" I asked, staring at the unappealing little creature.

She was sure! We named the kitten "*Gata*," which means cat in Spanish. Sam loved her baby kitty. Oh, how she tormented the poor thing! She carried her everywhere, and *Gata* never made a fuss; she'd go limp and let Sammy drag her around, dress her in doll clothes, and cuddle her to sleep. They were inseparable.

Gata lived a long life of over twenty years and grew into a beautiful specimen. Her fur glistened, and her markings were striking. The night she passed away was a sad occasion for our family. We'd gone away for a weekend of camping and returned to find her sprawled on the floor, unable to stand. I gently picked her up, wrapped her in a warm blanket, and held her in my arms while Mike called Samantha. When Sammy arrived, I handed *Gata* over, and she sat with *Gata* on her lap.

Speaking in a soft, soothing voice, she stroked her fur until sweet *Gata* drifted away. Sammy's first love was gone.

On the first day of kindergarten, Sam was bouncing with excitement. She couldn't wait to get going. *She was going to be a big kid, like her brother!* As we approached the classroom, she skipped into the room and wandered about curiously, examing everything in sight until she realized I was leaving. Crying, she wrapped her arms around my legs and pleaded with me. To calm her, I promised to stay a while. Once she finally settled down and was occupied with an activity, I quietly slipped out the door and made my way to work.

The first few days of school were stressful. Although Sammy was excited to go every morning and joyfully ran ahead of me to the classroom, she'd break down when I tried to leave. I was repeatedly late for work and felt torn between appeasing my angry employer and soothing my little girl.

Thankfully, Sammy eventually settled into the routine, but it wasn't long before we realized she was having difficulties. Sam didn't have a lot of interest in learning, but she loved interacting with other kids. She was easily distracted, wanted to spend all her time playing or talking with the other children, and became frustrated if she found a task trying. Miss. Thomas, her kindergarten teacher, starting sending home messages lamenting about Sam's lack of listening skills.

We were aware of the situation and becoming more and more concerned. When Sam worked on something, she'd get frustrated if she found it difficult. Sometimes, she'd stop and refuse to continue. She preferred to give up rather than keep trying. It was frustrating. I'd lose my patience with her, and she'd end up crying. However, I was optimistic she'd gain confidence. I hadn't cared for school at her age either. My report cards usually said I needed to get my head out of the clouds and focus because I was generally daydreaming rather than paying attention. It wasn't until grade four that I began to apply myself. Only after my handsome homeroom teacher told me I was smart.

Before the end of the school year, we had several meetings with Miss. Thomas, where we discussed whether Sammy should be held back. Miss Thomas, however, didn't think it was necessary, so Sam went into grade one.

We spent a great deal of time that summer helping Samantha with letters and numbers. She had difficulty staying on task and was easily overwhelmed. When practicing words, she'd usually cry. Often, she'd refuse to look at the book, and we'd end up fighting. My patience was short. It was horrible. She'd cry, and I'd yell. Those days were the closest I ever came to spanking her. It scared me, and I hated myself for it.

In September, Samantha started grade one. Both Mike and I were worried about what the year would hold. With Karl, we'd had similar concerns because Mrs. Halladay, the teacher, was a woman I felt had no business working with little children. She'd been a teacher for as long as I could remember, had even taught my sister. As a youth, I'd often seen her walking down the school hallway with her students while barking orders. Mrs. Halladay didn't seem to enjoy her job very much! I couldn't imagine she'd gotten softer with age. However, since Karl caught on to concepts quickly, it had worked out for him. We hoped it would be okay for Sammy even though I was fully aware of Mrs. Halladays tendency to show a preference for the easier students.

Grade one was difficult from the start. Sammy had a hard time following instructions, was slow to complete assignments in the allotted time frame, and struggled to keep up. There wasn't a teacher's aide available to spend extra time with her and help her understand. Mrs. Halladay responded by seeing Sam as lazy and difficult. When I spoke with Mrs. Halladay, she always complained about Sam's need for reassurance.

"Samantha doesn't pay attention, and I don't have the time to re-explain everything. She wants me to look at everything she does and tell her the next step."

Seeing Mrs. Halladay began to feel daunting; if she wasn't complaining about Sam's *laziness*, it was Sammy's fidgeting, her spending too much time in the bathroom, or sucking on her fingers. I often wondered if she had anything positive to report and quickly realized Sam must be struggling to interact with her. I was!

The school implemented an Individualized Program Plan (IPP) to set clear goals for Samantha's education. However, there were not a lot of actual educational goals in the plan. It consisted mostly of stopping her from sucking on her fingers and spending extra time in the bathroom. Naturally, Mike and I were also trying to break Sammy of the bad habits. Still, the IPP didn't feel appropriate for an educational plan. There were no steps in place to encourage Samantha. It was quickly apparent there wasn't a lot of tolerance towards her.

By the end of November, Samantha's desk had been moved to the front of the classroom, and she had been isolated from her peers. Mrs. Halladay felt it would allow Sam easier access to her without distracting the other students. Samantha was also placed in language therapy because she had difficulty differentiating between past, present, and future tense.

Within a month, the language therapist contacted me and encouraged us to have Samantha assessed. I had no idea that was an option! She explained that all children in Canada are entitled to an assessment to determine special needs. I was ecstatic by the news but unsure of how to proceed. "Contact Sam's teacher; she'll know what needs to be done," she said.

When I approached Mrs. Halladay and asked to have Samantha assessed, she looked at me in astonishment and said, "I don't know what you're asking. The school does not get involved or provide such things."

Confused, I reached out to the speech therapist, who encouraged me to pursue the matter and advocate for Samantha. She told me to approach our family physician and go back to Mrs. Halladay and request a psychoeducational assessment. "Tell her you know the school has to arrange for one if requested."

Somewhat apprehensive about pursuing the matter, I discussed Samantha's struggles with our family doctor. She immediately referred Sammy for neurological testing and confirmed the speech therapist's claim. Each school board is responsible for allocating resources for special needs students. In Canada, psychoeducational assessments cost an average of $2,000–$3,500. Parents can, of course, pay for the review if they wish. However, we didn't have the money to do so. We were a young couple, both working but barely making ends meet.

Armed with the information, I again reached out to Mrs. Halladay. However, she wouldn't return my phone calls. Frustrated, I left work early several days in a row, hoping to have a face-to-face with her. Foolishly, it never even occurred to me to discuss the matter with anyone other than Sam's teacher. I didn't want to step on anyone's toes and accidentally make matters more difficult for Sam, who by now had been labelled the "problem child."

Samantha's classmates had been instructed to call her out and tell her to stop sucking her fingers when they saw her with them in her mouth. Everyone was encouraged to talk to her loud enough for the whole class to hear. *Imagine that you're a six-year-old struggling to fit in and intimidated by the teacher. Now, add classmates who have been told to publicly shame you.*

The next few months were a game of cat and mouse. I'd walk into the school and lurk through the hallways trying to get a moment with Mrs. Halladay, who hastily turned in the opposite direction. When I was able to speak with her, she had plenty of reasons for not yet knowing if Samantha would receive the psychoeducational assessment.

"I haven't had time to look into your question about the special testing. I still don't have an answer for you." Or sometimes she'd say, "It's been a busy time for me."

When I asked her to complete the school portion of questions from Dr. Lewis, the neurologist working on Sammy's evaluation, she was reluctant.

"Oh, this will take time; it's rather large!"

"He needs it back by the end of the month," I replied.

When the month ended, I requested the completed paperwork, but she dodged my calls. One afternoon, I marched into the school to confront her and found Samantha sitting directly outside her classroom door.

"What are you doing here? Why aren't you in class?"

"I have to sit here," Sammy replied and went back to carefully tracing the letters in her workbook.

Soon, it became a regular occurrence to find Sammy sitting in the hallway rather than the classroom. I didn't want to jump to conclusions, but it seemed her desk had been moved permanently. *How is a child expected to learn while working alone outside of her class? How is a child supposed to make friends when they have been instructed to single her out? How does a little girl who is already struggling manage to go to school every day when she is repeatedly isolated and made to feel inadequate?*

Exasperated, Mike and I decided I needed to quit my job to monitor what was happening in the school. We couldn't afford for me not to work, but Samantha's wellbeing was our priority. So, I started going to school every single day. Mrs. Halladay began to visibly flinch at the sight of me.

"The paperwork isn't done yet, and I'm still looking into getting Samantha assessed. It's very expensive, and we're not sure we can afford it," she said.

"Okay, I'll stop in tomorrow," I replied.

Finally, after months of stalking Sam's teacher, Mrs. Halladay grudgingly informed me a referral had been submitted. By then, half of the school year had passed, and Sammy had become obsessive. Her desk was pristine; she disliked any dirt and compulsively organized her bedroom. When I helped her with school work, she erased and re-erased every tiny mistake, spending an excessive amount of time making her letters perfect. Her printing had to be immaculate. Any little mark on her paper brought her to tears. We didn't know how to help her relax. It was hard to watch. At night, we helped her study the weekly sight words. We'd go over them until she was scoring ten out of ten, but she'd go to school and take the test, only to fail and come home disheartened. She stopped trying new activities; if she thought something looked difficult, she wouldn't do it. Unless she knew she could do something perfectly, she didn't want to try.

That January, after months of waiting, Samantha finally had the first part of the psychoeducational assessment, the Wechsler Intelligence Scale (WISC-III), a standard test that's initial version was developed in 1949. A chartered psychologist went to the school and administered the test. It was a long and tedious evaluation process, and the results took a long time to come in.

In mid-June, we met with Mrs. Halladay, the school principal and the examiner. The WISC results showed Sam scoring below the tenth percentile in reading and math. She was significantly delayed and fell at an early to mid-kindergarten level. Her comprehension was a two on a scale where the average score was eight–twelve. She had difficulty with short-term auditory memory, deductive visual reasoning, and common sense. Sammy seemed to do better when there were accompanying pictures or other visual cues. She struggled with verbal reasoning and practical judgment. However, overall she was functioning in a mild to EMH (educable mentally handicap) range of intellectual deficiency.

As they spoke, I looked at Mike, who appeared as shocked and confused as I felt. "What do you mean by mentally handicapped?" was the only question I managed to utter.

"What it means is that although Sam will continue to learn, she will learn at a slower rate than other students, and as she matures, she will likely fall further and further behind."

"How far behind?"

There was a moment, then a deep sigh. "It's likely that Sam will require modifications to help her succeed. She'll need a lot of repetition and will probably learn better with pictures, additional instruction, having her paraphrase what's she's heard, and constant review."

"How far behind?" I repeated.

The examiner locked eyes with me first, then Mike. "Sam will fall significantly behind. She will not be able to keep up with a regular curriculum. It's likely she won't hold down a regular job or function the way you and I do. You will need to make modifications for her and accept her limitations."

My heart was pounding. *What were they saying?* Their words weren't making any sense!

"What do you mean she won't have a regular job? She is six years old! How can you possibly tell us she can't have a job? None of this makes sense. Sammy is having a hard time, but she can do lots of things. You are not describing a girl I recognize." I objected with rising panic.

Once again, there was a moment of silence before the reply, "She'll be able to work, but it'll need to be a repetitive job, something like an assembly line or gas jockey."

I felt they were telling us to give up on her future. They were placing limitations on her abilities, and I was shell-shocked. When I looked at Mike, his eyes were glossy. We reached for each other's hand and squeezed. *How could this be happening?* I knew she was having difficulties, and I understood she was a handful, but the girl they described was severely handicapped, and Sammy didn't appear handicapped to me!

Mike and I walked out of that meeting in disbelief. *What was her future going to look like? How could we help her? Was it truly hopeless?*

As I reached for the door handle, Mrs. Halladay grabbed my arm and said. "You were right; Samantha needed to be evaluated. Now that I've seen the results, I understand why you insisted. I thought she was just defiant, but she has severe problems I wasn't aware of."

I flinched back. I detested that woman. She had singled Sammy out, isolated her, berated her, allowed and encouraged bullying. She had made my six-year-old child's life miserable, fought me at every turn, and refused to get Sam the help she needed.

That evening, Mike and I sat in silence, each wrestling our fears. We were bewildered, yoyoing between rage, disbelief, and resistance. *How could they possibly predict her future? How could they be positive that the gaps in learning would increase with age?* As I flipped through her baby book, tears rolled down my cheeks. I wanted a diagnosis. What exactly caused the cognitive disability? Perhaps the neurological results would tell us, but I had no idea when those results would be in.

CHAPTER 5

The Snake Within

The Wagner's were a relatively new family to our community. They lived on a large acreage at the edge of town on a property consisting of a main house and a second smaller home, which they rented out.

Reni Wagner was a friendly, soft-spoken woman who seemed attentive to her children. I didn't know her very well—most of our interactions were during school field trips or parent advisory groups. She was always busy, running from commitment to commitment, working the family-owned business, and volunteering at the school. They had two children, a boy, Travis, in Karl's grade, and a girl, Josie, one grade above Sam. Travis and Karl spent a lot of time together and often visited each other's homes.

Reni formed a monthly dinner club and invited us to join. The club was made of several couples, and each pair hosted a themed dinner once a month. The first time Mike and I attended, it was hosted at the Wagner home. Normally, children didn't participate, but they were having a family barbeque. The day was warm, the sun was shining, and a light breeze gently rustled the trees. Karl and Samantha were thrilled to spend the afternoon running around and jumping on the trampoline with other children.

Mr. Wagner was an odd man and somewhat standoffish. He had a tendency to start preaching at the drop of a hat, which made me a little uncomfortable. His abrupt shift from joking to deep religious conversations, followed by an angry kick towards the family cat, bothered me. I've never cared much for people who are cruel to animals. However, in the spirit of being neighbourly, we met for brunch and attended the monthly dinners on several occasions.

One Saturday afternoon, the Wagner's invited our family for lunch. Afterwards, as Mike and I prepared to leave, Josie asked Samantha to spend the night. Travis was having a sleepover at our house. Sam had never spent a lot of time away from home, so at first, we said no, but Sammy was so excited that we eventually gave in. Heading out the door with Karl and Travis, we kissed Sammy on the cheek and left.

The boys watched Disney movies, played Pokemon, and went to sleep around ten. The next morning, I dropped off Travis and picked up Samantha. Once home, Karl and Samantha played, and all was fine until evening. I was sitting on Sammy's bed, braiding her hair, and she hesitantly whispered, "Mommy, Josie touched my vagina." Concerned that either of my children would ever experience sexual assault, I'd taught them the correct terminology at a very young age.

Sammy's words stopped me in my tracks. Cautiously, I took a deep breath and willed calm into my voice. "What do you mean, honey?" *Breathe, keep your voice calm, don't get angry, smile gently. No matter what, don't frighten her!*

Wide-eyed, Sammy looked down and pointed between her legs. "I didn't want her to, but she said it would be fun."

"I see . . . did anything else happen?"

"No."

"Okay, it's alright. Thank you for telling me." I answered and gently tucked her into bed.

That night was sleepless. My mind kept racing. *What should I do?*

❧

The following morning, as Sammy sat for breakfast, she looked up at me and said, "She kissed me," and pointed down.

"Whe . . . where?" I stammered.

"My vagina, and she smelled my panties. Ugh . . . ugh . . . she said they smelled good."

My breath was coming in short, shallow gasps. I felt my stomach turning, fear gripping my chest. *This is much more than childish curiosity; this is perverse.*

"Josie said it was a secret. Why did she do that, Mommy? I didn't like it, and now she's gonna be mad at me cuz it's a secret."

Keep calm, don't get agitated! I thought. Taking a deep breath and nodding, I tried to reassure her. "It's okay, honey, you didn't do anything wrong. You were right to tell me."

Sam's eyes were wide with worry. "Why did she did she do that?"

My mind was racing. *How the hell did this happen?* Followed by, *Oh my God, the first half of Samantha's psychoeducation assessment is this morning. What do I do?* We'd been on the waiting list since the year before, and Dr. Lewis was finally sending someone to the school. It was too late to cancel; they were already on their way! Filled with dread, I took Sammy to school, kissed her, and wished her a good day, knowing full well it probably wasn't going to be.

She was worried. "What if Josie wants to do that again? Is she gonna be mad at me?"

I drove home and spent the morning pacing, unsure of what to do. Sam's voice kept running through my head. *Josie said it would be fun . . . said it would be fun . . . said it would be fun. She touched and kissed . . . touched and kissed. Children don't randomly molest each other!* I concluded and dialed Reni Wagner's number.

"Morning, how are you?" she asked.

Taking a deep breath and gathering my courage, I cautiously responded, "Not great—we need to talk."

She fell silent as I relayed Samantha's story. "Reni, children don't make this kind of thing up, and it doesn't sound like kids being curious. I think Josie might have been molested." The words tumbled out of my mouth.

Stunned, Reni took a deep breath and told me she'd been molested as a child. "I think you might be right," she added with concern in her voice.

"How well do you know your renters?" I questioned, not wanting to make accusations but grasping for a possible culprit. Statistically, most children are molested by someone known to the family, and they lived on an acreage. Also, Josie didn't spend time in town. It had to be someone close to her, someone with easy access. I felt sure of it. Something had happened to her. The words and gestures Sammy used when describing the incident sounded adult.

Reni replied, "We don't know them very well, but they seem nice, and the kids sometimes visit them. Umm, I need to talk to Josie. I'll get back to you." Abruptly, she hung up.

The days dragged on as I waited to hear from Reni, but she didn't call. My concern for Sam's state of mind and Josie's safety weighed heavily. On several occasions, I picked up the phone and started to contact Reni, only to change my mind and hang up. I didn't want to add to her worry.

Finally, she called, but not about the girls. "Hi, we'd like to have a Mexican-themed dinner and wondered if you'd host it?" I was taken aback and testily wondered out loud if she'd spoken to Josie. Sammy was all I could think about. She was having trouble sleeping; she was confused. She wanted to be

Josie's friend but didn't want to do *that* again. "What if Josie is mad at me for telling? What if she doesn't want to be my friend anymore?" Mike and I were considering having Sam see a counsellor.

"Oh, yes. Everything is great. She hasn't been abused," Reni cheerfully replied, then quickly switched the topic back to the Mexican supper.

"What did Josie say?" I prodded.

"Just that she hasn't been touched."

"What about what happened with Sam?"

"Oh, she promised Doug it won't happen again."

"What do you mean? Weren't you there?"

"No, Doug preferred to handle it," she quickly replied.

I was furious. *How could Reni let Doug talk to her alone? Why wouldn't she insist on being a part of the conversation?*

In frustration, I snapped. "There is no way I would ever let Mike talk to Sammy alone. A daughter needs her mother. Don't you think you should have been there?"

"Well . . . yes, but Doug felt it was best if he spoke to her alone," she retorted defensively.

I hung up the phone, bewildered and angry. My stomach was in knots. Feeling uneasy, I called my friend Diana. I needed to bounce my fears off someone. "Am I being paranoid?" I wondered, and she reassured me I wasn't. So, later that day, I reported the incident to family services. My instincts kept screaming at me—*it needs to be investigated.* The social worker I spoke with told me she needed to interview the children and would do so at the school. I asked if I should let Doug and Reni know beforehand. I didn't think they should be blindsided, but the social worker told me not to call them.

I didn't feel comfortable with Sam being interviewed without me but supposedly *it was better for the child.*

For the next few days, I walked on eggshells. *Had I done the right thing? Was it really appropriate to not let the Wagner's know what I'd done? Did I want Samantha to relive the experience by talking it out with a stranger?* It was pointless to stress; there was nothing I could do to stop the wheels I'd set in motion.

On the day of the interview, Reni called me. I expected anger from her, but instead, she was hurt. "Why would you report this? Doug already dealt with it," she reproached. The conversation was conflicting; hurting people always makes me feel guilty. Still, I wondered if she was in a state of denial. I was hopeful that family services would investigate, but all they did was interview Josie, and that was the end of it. So Mike and I kept our distance from the Wagner's.

During Christmas break, I received another phone call from Reni. "Why aren't we friends anymore? We're hurt that you've stopped coming to dinners and no longer want to visit," she stated. "Is it because of what happened with the kids? It was all a misunderstanding, and we'd like you to come for Christmas brunch."

I didn't want to go, but I felt guilty. *What if I was being paranoid? What if my mistrust of Doug was clouding my judgment?* Doubt about my misgivings always was a sure way to make me conform, so I cautiously agreed to go.

We arrived to an elaborately set table filled with all the traditional Christmas goodies. Lunch was quiet. I was uneasy and kept a close eye on the whereabouts of my kids. After lunch, Doug and Reni presented us with a gift. It was a Christmas book.

"Would you mind if I read a few passages?" Doug asked and proceeded to read about Jesus's birth. Mike and I sat in silence until he was done. "Do you believe Jesus was born to bring peace and forgiveness?" Doug asked. Surprised, Mike and I glanced at one another then proceeded to nod.

"We do, too, which is why we want to put the past behind us and move forward in our friendship," Doug stated, as Reni nodded in agreement. "Can we do that?"

The conversation was awkward. It felt rehearsed and false. *How could we move forward?* I didn't trust him and couldn't wait to get out of there, so we quickly gathered our children and left.

As the year went on, Mike and I tried to keep our distance, although I spoke with Reni on several occasions. When the family made the decision to move to another province, she stopped in for tea.

"How are the kids?" I asked.

"They are good, Travis is at home, and Doug took Josie with him to build the fence on the new property. They'll be back next week," she cheerfully responded.

My heart stopped. "Why would Doug take Josie instead of Travis? Doesn't it make more sense to take Travis? He's older, and he's a boy," I snapped.

Fidgetting, Reni avoided my gaze and replied. "I know what your thinking, and you're wrong."

CHAPTER 6

New Beginnings

I don't necessarily believe experts are always right. Science, while incredibly valuable, doesn't take into account the human spirit. As a young girl, I was acutely introverted. I was shy to the extreme; it was excruciating trying to form relationships. I remember adults always saying, "Cat got your tongue?" It's such a horrible expression! I found it demeaning and insulting because it often felt like something *did* have my tongue. Speaking was chest constricting. Words struggled to come out, and I felt ridiculed.

Every time I responded to a question, I recall having difficulty focusing. So I retreated into a fantasy world of daydreams, happier within my imagination. Often, when I managed to form friendships, others easily took advantage of me. I didn't have the necessary self-esteem to say no because I was desperate to be liked.

My early years of school were difficult. In many ways, I was like Samantha. It was easier to withdraw than to fail while trying! Fortunately, throughout my youth, there were several teachers along the way who believed in my potential. It's truly amazing how much other people's perceptions can influence our lives. So, as Sam's mom, I refused to accept the limitations placed upon her. I was determined to nurture her strengths and help her see her amazing potential.

Part of nurturing Sam's growth involved hiring tutors and encouraging her participation in activities she excelled at, such as dance and swimming, regardless of financial strain. We hired her first tutor the summer after what I felt was the nightmare of grade one and continued off and on throughout the years.

That summer, when she wasn't meeting with the tutor, she was playing in the backyard with her brother, swimming, riding her bike, or camping. She was relaxed, happier than she'd been all year, comfortable, trusting, and innocent.

When September came around and grade two started, we worried. *What would the next year look like for Sam?* We met with Mrs. Miller a week after the school year began; both of us were eager to develop an agreed-upon plan for the year. From the first meeting, we were pleasantly surprised.

Mrs. Miller introduced herself and immediately stated, "Samantha is a sweet, gentle little girl; she's not at all what I expected." Reaching into her desk, she produced a piece of paper with Samantha's name and handed it to Mike.

"Before starting, the staff briefed me on my students. This is the information I received on Samantha."

The paper had two columns; one side listed Samantha's weaknesses and the other her strengths. The negative column was lengthy. It catalogued her need for constant reassurance, the requests for many bathroom breaks, excessive time frames for completing assignments, sucking on her fingers, unwillingness to participate in class, open defiance, fidgeting, and classroom disruption. The positive side listed two items—she had a charming smile and enjoyed art. I was outraged. My blood ran cold. Even after the psychoeducational assessment, which explained Sam's cognitive struggles, Mrs. Halladay's dislike for Sam was apparent.

Throughout the second grade, Sammy slowly started to emerge from her shell. She was doing much better, felt more comfortable, and started to enjoy her classes. Mrs. Miller worked closely with Sam, and Sam flourished with the positive feedback. Through regular communication, Mrs. Miller kept us informed and together, we worked at helping Sam be successful. However, Sam's need for frequent reassurance continued, and she still relied on sucking her middle fingers for comfort. Mike and I kept trying to break her of the habit, but it wasn't easy. It was a defence mechanism she resorted to when stressed or tired. Her teeth started twisting and coming in crooked, which caused her embarrassment. Sometimes, she refused to smile. She was extremely self-conscious. Eventually, the dentist implanted a small roller on the roof of her mouth, which made inserting her fingers in her mouth uncomfortable, so she was forced to stop the habit. By the end of grade two, Samantha no longer inserted her fingers in her mouth. Unfortunately, although Sam was happier, some classmates continued to single her out. The pattern from the previous year was tricky to curve.

That October, we finally received the results from the neurological assessment. Dr. Lewis noted Samantha's dramatic improvement based on Mrs. Millers' feedback and the contrast to previous year's input. Dr. Lewis explained Sam's difficulty concentrating and said she had some mild motor-skill impairments. She also had trouble with short-term memory but was able to retain information with repetition. Her printing was slow. She had a tendency to hold her pencil tightly and with considerable pressure, which caused her hand to cramp.

We asked about ADHD, but he didn't think Sam had a significant attention weakness, at least not one that would warrant a diagnosis. He suggested auditory, visual, and tactile approaches when presenting instructions, dependant on the task. He recommended Samantha take part in the activities she felt confident about at least three times per week.

"She loves dancing and swimming," I piped in.

"Good, she should do those kinds of activities."

The conversation was far more encouraging than the one we'd had at the end of grade one. However, there wasn't a definitive diagnosis, and I desperately wanted one. I had hoped for something to point my finger at, but the results didn't answer all the questions. *Why was she so impulsive? Why was forming friendships so difficult? How could we make others understand that she wasn't just rude or defiant? What could we do to help her?* I thought if she had a diagnosis, I would accept her limitations, but there was no specific reason, and I remained at a loss, disheartened and worried about her future.

Many evenings, I'd lie awake, wondering how we could help Sammy, secretly blaming myself for her struggles. *Was I responsible because of the anxiety and stress I'd experienced while expecting her? Was it because I sometimes suffered from depression? Was it genetic?* However, when I voiced my concerns to the experts, they always assured me there wasn't a specific factor to blame.

Although Samantha continued to improve in school throughout that year, social cues remained a problem. Boundaries were often a difficult concept for her. More often than not, she and Karl fought. She loved to push his buttons and intrude upon his personal space by "borrowing" his possessions. Her behavior unpredictable, she often said the first thing that popped into her mind, regardless of the consequences. She didn't seem to understand my explanations regarding appropriate behaviours and was too friendly.

Mike and I owned a towing company, and once a bailiff stopped by the house to pick up a repossessed car Mike had towed. As I gathered the paperwork and went outside, I found Sam standing beside his vehicle, chatting away amiably. She was always striking conversations with strangers. *This frightened me!* I frequently instructed her to stay away from strangers and often worried about the fine line between scaring her and keeping her safe. As the bailiff prepared to leave, he warned. "I used to be a police officer. Be careful. Your daughter is much too trusting."

The next year, Samantha began to regress once more. Teasing from other students increased. Often, others took Sam's possessions from her desk. Name-calling and being excluded from games during recess occurred daily. It was frustrating. I longed to protect her but also wanted her to fight her own battles.

As other students started reading more advanced stories, some began making fun of Sam for not reading as well. This, combined with her need for additional time to complete assignments, increased Sam's feelings of self-doubt. At home, she often cried and said she was dumb and ugly. She began covering her mouth when talking or smiling, and she stopped wearing ponytails because she believed her ears were too big.

As the bullying increased, I felt powerless to help. I was angry not only about Sam's bullying but about everything! Our family business was floundering. The following spring, when we fell seriously behind on our mortgage, I nailed a "For Sale" sign to the fence. Within a month, we sold our family home and were homeless. We stored our remaining possessions and moved into our holiday trailer until we found an acreage with a small cabin for rent.

Anger and bitterness increased the amount of fighting between Mike and me. We were constantly screaming at each other, words that no couple should ever say to one another. In retrospect, I realize I blamed him for our business failure and having to sell our home, a place I'd loved and hoped to raise our family in. Life felt out of control.

Desperate to regain some sort of authority in life, I applied for the full-time program to complete the accounting diploma I'd been working towards. That's probably the only intelligent decision I made that year. I was on a downward spiral, depressed and angry about our financial struggles and headed down a self-destructive path of heavy drinking during the weekends.

Unable to regulate my emotions, I fluctuated between being too hard on the kids and not hard enough. Karl was much easier to relate to than Sam. Karl didn't want to disappoint; he listened to the rules. Sam, however, was headstrong, excitable, and impulse-driven. She and I were always butting heads. It was difficult for me to communicate with her, and I hated myself for it. Sometimes I didn't want to be around any of my family. Life overwhelmed me. My inner dialogue was destructive. I started telling myself they were better off without me. Death was often on my mind.

Depression is a funny thing; it plays havoc with not only emotions but also thoughts. I told myself I was an utter failure. My marriage was failing, we were broke, and I didn't know how to parent my two completely opposite children. Living with my secret shame, I tried to maintain a semblance of normalcy. Miraculously, I forced myself to complete the accounting diploma, but I hit rock bottom once that was done.

Mike and I separated the following spring. I moved into my friend Diana's spare room and focused on finding a place for the kids and me to live. I cut myself off from my family and refused to speak to my mom, who blamed me for the separation. It was a desolate time of pain and self-reproach.

During the summer months, Mike and I got back together and decided to repair our marriage. It was a long road, and my depression made it even more difficult. The self-destructive dialogue I replayed in my mind led to a failed suicide attempt, followed by months of therapy and deep self-examination.

Worried about Sam's upcoming academic year, we decided to send her to a school with better resources for children with learning disabilities. Once we chose the school, we bought a small acreage and made plans to relocate our small family. The move was emotional for me. I'd grown up in the community we were leaving, and I'd loved living there. Also, Karl had done well there. He had many friends, and I felt guilty about uprooting him, but Mike and I knew Samantha would never flourish there. They didn't have the funding needed for her growth or the desire to make accommodations for students like her. Plus, we needed a fresh start to work on our marriage. We'd had a difficult time and felt the change might be good for the whole family.

CHAPTER 7

Someone Else's Life

Oh, the joy of seeing my little girl happy, with friends, engaged, and looking forward to her classes. We understood she would always have difficulties, but she was trying her best, and it'd been a long time since she'd said she was stupid.

Her anxiety about school had lessened. She enjoyed the social aspect of her daily routine, had several friends, and was becoming quite the social butterfly, often fluttering between classmates. She'd even developed a deep friendship with a classmate who took the same school bus. Her teacher was encouraging, communicated regularly with us, and showed patience and understanding. She had requested a new psychoeducational assessment, and I hadn't even asked for it. So, I allowed myself the luxury of relaxing a little.

As a whole, the family seemed to be doing better. Mike and I were no longer fighting, and I continued working with my therapist. Sam was having regular school counselling, which was definitely improving her self-esteem. Karl was in his first year of junior high and was adjusting to the change. Life was good.

Of course, the move wasn't a miracle cure. There were issues, but they were minor in comparison to the previous years. Sam was still having some playground squabbles and had difficulty with social cues. She occasionally complained about other students, but she was doing well academically, had many new friends, was learning restraint and became less bossy. It was wonderful! We felt we'd made the right decision for her; even having her repeat the third grade had been right. She was doing so much better!

I answered the telephone on the third ring. It was Ruby's mom. Sam and Ruby were friends at school. They'd been friends since the year before. Ruby had invited Sammy to her birthday party, and we'd had Ruby over on a few occasions.

We exchanged hellos, and then Ruby's mother launched into a cautious explanation for the late evening call. It was a call I never expected to receive during my lifetime! The things she was saying weren't making sense. *Obviously, it was some sort of crazy joke.*

Ruby had confessed a secret to her mother. A couple of girls in Sammy's fourth-grade class had approached her and some other classmates. They were actively recruiting friends into a secret club with one purpose. They wanted the group to follow Samantha after school as she walked to her grand-parent's home and beat her up. But they didn't just want to beat her up, they wanted to beat her *to death*!

How does one react to such a conversation? My legs felt oddly weak, my hand clenched the phone with a death grip, a nervous titter of denial escaped my lips, followed by a long gasp as I fought for air to fill my lungs.

"What do you mean they want to kill her?" *This is a joke!* I thought. *She must've had a fight with one of the girls. I want to kill her, would have been said out of frustration. It was a common phrase! It didn't mean anything. People say crazy things all the time. They're kids!* "What do you mean they want to kill her?" I shakily repeated.

Apparently, Ruby had arrived home withdrawn and sullen. Something was weighing heavily on her mind. After a lot of questions from her mother, she'd broken down. For several weeks, two girls in her class had been putting pressure on her. Every day she'd said no, but now it was becoming hard to refuse. Several girls had agreed to join the "club," and Ruby was worried; she couldn't keep the secret anymore. There was a plan. They wanted to follow Sam after school. Sam often walked two blocks to her grandparent's house. They felt with enough club members, Sam wouldn't be able to get away.

As she spoke, the room began to spin. *Is this happening?* Surely, I was in a nightmare, about to wake up at any moment, and life would go back to normal. *This conversation couldn't be real. They were children. Things like this only happened in the movies.* Only this wasn't a movie, and I was standing in my kitchen, learning about a plot to kill my little girl.

Everything seemed to slow down, so I focused on breathing as she spoke. I wanted desperately to believe if I blinked hard enough, the world would right itself and start spinning again. As the voice on the other end of the phone began to distort in my ear, I tried to concentrate. Ruby's mother was saying she'd let the school know in the morning. She assured me Ruby would answer all questions truthfully. I weakly thanked her in a strangled voice and hung up.

Afterwards, I went about the evening routine of making lunches and getting the kids organized for bed. Once they were safely in their rooms, I slowly walked to the living room and whispered the details of the conversation to Mike. His incredulous look matched my feelings of surrealism. It was unfathomable. Little girls talking murder! *They're just kids. They can't really mean it. Oh, my God, they want to hurt Samantha. No . . . no, it must be a mistake. What if it's not a mistake? What do we do?* The thoughts running through my mind kept me up all night.

The next morning, I sent Karl on the bus and Samantha to her grandparents for the day, then I called the school. Mrs. Andrews, the school principal, was taken aback. I could hear her disbelief as I described my phone call with Ruby's mom. I understood her confusion; I'd experienced the same doubt the previous night. We were talking about young children, but it didn't matter that they were in fourth grade. Kids have killed kids. Adults aren't the only one who commit murder, and these girls had a plan!

We kept Sammy home for the rest of the week while Mrs. Andrews made arrangements to interview the girls. Days of silence went by, so I reached out to the school again.

The children had been interviewed, and parents were notified. None of the girls had confessed, but Ruby had remained true to her version. Still, Mrs. Andrews was confident it'd been handled.

Once Sam went back to school, we stopped allowing her to walk anywhere; instead, I picked her up and dropped her off every day. We didn't tell her the reason for the change in routine. We didn't want to frighten her, but she found out anyway. Ruby told her about the plan as soon as she went back to school.

That evening, Sam came home with tears rolling down her face. She wanted to know why they hated her. "I thought they were my friends." Sam sobbed.

"I know my girl," I replied as I held her in my arms and stroked her hair. "I promise you, baby, everything is going to be alright. I'll never let anything happen to you. No matter what."

As the weeks progressed, Sam became increasingly anxious. She didn't want to go to school—the girls were watching her every move. She felt vulnerable, unsafe, and exposed. Every night we tried to calm her, but she had trouble falling asleep and often woke during the night. Every morning, I reassured her that one of us would pick her up after school. She was eight years old and in constant fear!

As an English-speaking child attending a Mexican school, I'm familiar with bullies. I vividly recall hiding from some girls in a bathroom stall, afraid for my wellbeing, but I never feared for my life, so I can't even begin to imagine how Sammy felt.

The school believed they had dealt with the matter because they were closely watching all the girls. However, girls can be extremely subtle when they want to be. They add a form of psychological warfare into the mix; their methods often don't involve fists. Looks, whispers, and snide laughter can cause tremendous anxiety and chip away at self-esteem. Just watch a group of girls playing together. All too often, one girl becomes the outcast, usually the one who isn't quite a part of the group, but at first glance, it's not obvious.

I contacted the school once more and demanded a meeting with school officials and the parents of the two children who came up with the plan and began recruiting the others. I explained, "Sammy is still being bullied."

The school was hesitant to further pursue the matter. In their view, the problem was over, but I insisted, so they agreed to contact the parents. It was a couple of days before they scheduled a meeting. Both Mike and I were eager to meet the parents, so we arrived early and waited.

When we sat down with Mrs. Andrews, I began by asking about the other parents. "Regrettably, they called this morning. They won't be coming."

I was mad. "Why not?"

"They've spoken with their daughters, and both say the girls are staying away from Sam. The matter has been handled."

"How can they say that? Their daughters were planning to attack Samantha. Their daughters are still bullying her."

"What are they doing?"

There it was . . . *what were they doing?* They were glaring, whispering, following Sam with their gaze. But they were cautious about their aggression. I tried to explain the situation and expressed our deep concern and Sam's fear, but outwardly the girls were behaving themselves.

"Mrs. Proulx, I understand your concerns, but they're only children," Mrs. Andrews replied. It was obvious she was desperately clinging to the belief that children don't hurt one another. I understood her need to believe that. I wanted to believe it as well.

"Forgive me, Mrs. Andrews, but I'm afraid you might be wrong. I don't think we can be sure of anything, and now they are angry at Sam because they got into trouble. They make Sam uncomfortable. The bullying has not stopped, and let's face it; kids have killed kids." My voice was nearing hysteria; my fear was palpable. I knew I sounded dramatic, and trying to explain the stares made me sound a little foolish.

Mrs. Andrews blinked and said, "I understand, but we can't do anything about stares and whispers. We need something concrete."

Mike, always the steady voice of reason in our marriage, took my hand as my voice began to rise. Calmly he told Mrs. Andrews we would be contacting the police and reporting the incident.

"We understand they're children, but they made a plan to hurt Samantha, and she is afraid." He remained steady. We knew the police wouldn't take us seriously, either, but it was a threat, the only threat we could make.

When we left the office, we were frustrated. How could they possibly expect us to let it go and continue to send our daughter to the school where her life had been threatened?

How could we feel comfortable if the parents of the girls involved weren't willing to even discuss the incident with us?

The next morning, Mrs. Andrews called. "Both parents have decided to send their daughters to another school. They don't want any further problems, and the girls will be leaving tomorrow."

I was relieved when the two girls transferred to the school across town. It meant they wouldn't have access to Sammy, but I also worried. *What if the remaining girls decided to hurt Sam anyway? Could the two instigating girls walk across town and hurt Sam with a whole new group of girls? We would keep a close eye on Sammy, just in case!*

CHAPTER 8

Code Of Conduct

The rest of the school year was better. Sam went to weekly school counselling sessions and developed a great rapport with the counsellor. It did her a lot of good, and once more, she started to enjoy school.

Since growing up on an acreage can be quite lonely, we involved both Karl and Sammy in various activities. Sam was in dance, swam, attended youth groups, and played school sports. I often felt like a taxi driver.

Dance was Sam's true passion. She loved to perform! Her dedication to practice was inspiring. She'd spend hours blaring music from her room and going over her routines. When she wasn't practicing, she was choreographing her own moves. She kept a binder full of choreographed dances and often put on a show for Mike and me. Whether she was dancing in the living room or on a stage with the rest of her class, her face glowed with pure joy! Dancing was her outlet, her form of expression, the one activity she couldn't be without.

Sam had deep compassion and genuine empathy for all creatures. She hated seeing any animal in distress and cried if she found an injured bird or rabbit and regularly brought home strays to nurse back to health. Once Sam witnessed our German Sheppard kill a muskrat and became hysterical. Another time, she jumped in between our dog and a stray cat during a fight. Sam was trying to protect the cat. Luckily, she didn't get hurt.

When Sam was in grade five, she developed a passion for horses. She had spent some time on Diana's farm riding with her daughter, so when Diana told me she was selling their old 4H horse, Bonus, we bought her. Sammy loved that horse; she'd rush home after school and immediately run outside to spend hours with her. Sam loved riding, brushing, and confiding in Bonus. Their bond was special, which would prove valuable during another difficult year.

That same year, the school hired a new counsellor; the previous counsellor had moved to another school. I knew the change would be difficult for Sammy, so when Mr. Monrow started, I immediately contacted him with a brief rundown on Sam's history.

Teddy Munrow was young, a recent graduate. He was short in stature, rotund, with spiky black hair and flamboyance. His friendly demeanour placed me at ease. *Sam will be fine with him.*

Samantha had weekly sessions with Mr. Monrow, and at first they seemed to be going well. As was my habit, I was actively involved, often volunteered at the school, and regularly checked in with her teachers and Mr. Monrow.

One afternoon as I was heading out the door after helping out in the classroom, Mr. Monrow intercepted me. Testily, he said Samantha had taken a pencil from his desk during one of their sessions. I was mortified, quickly apologized, and assured him I would be talking with her. I've never had illusions that my children were saints; most kids do bad things at one point or another.

That evening, I confronted Samantha about stealing. She firmly denied it. No matter how many ways I tried to get a confession, she stuck to her guns and insisted she was innocent. Sam wasn't a good liar. Oh, she tried, but we always knew when she wasn't telling the truth; she had sure telltale signs. Her eye avoidance and fidgeting always gave her away. However, none of the signs were there, and I wasn't sure how to proceed. She was so adamant! Still, I didn't doubt Mr. Monrow, so I grounded her.

The next week, I again bumped into Mr. Monrow. He immediately brought up the topic of his missing pencil. He was visibly upset about it.

"We've grounded her, but Sammy says she didn't take it," I replied.

"She did," he vehemently responded.

Surprised, I asked, "Did you see her take it?"

"No, but she took it."

"How can you be sure it was her?" I wondered.

"I noticed it missing right after Sam left my office. It was definitely her. She owes me an apology."

I was offended. Sam had never stolen anything before, although it certainly didn't mean she hadn't done it this time. Mr. Monrow was so sure, but Sam was equally determined, so I told him I'd talk to her.

That evening, I spoke with Sam again. It was a loud conversation. Sam insisted she hadn't done it. The more I tried to talk to her, the more she denied it and the angrier she became.

"It's not fair. I didn't do it!"

When I demanded she apologize to Mr. Monrow, she lost it.

"I won't; you can't make me. I didn't take it, and I won't apologize," she screamed.

A few days later, Mr. Monrow approached me. I told him that although Sam had been punished, she refused to apologize. He was angry and said, "It was her. She needs to take ownership and apologize!"

Suspiciously, I retorted, "Have you spoken to her about taking your pencil?"

"No, I haven't," he responded.

Taken aback, I wondered out loud, "Why haven't you asked her about it?"

"Huh . . . are you and your husband having problems at home?" Mr. Monrow spat.

"No . . . why?" I replied defensively.

"Perhaps Sam's difficulties are a result of a volatile environment," he retorted, while crossing his arms and raising his eyebrows.

"We are not having problems at home," I responded. He was making me feel defensive!

Shrugging his shoulders, he knowingly smirked at me. My skin prickled. I felt judged, but I forced myself to shrug it off. *He's just exploring all options. It's his job to look out for the students. Don't be so sensitive.*

As days went on, Samantha continued to complain about Mr. Monrow. Based on her comments, I was getting the sense he didn't like Samantha very much, but I assumed he'd remain impartial and professional. When Samantha and Ruby began having squabbles, both girls sought advice from Mr. Monrow. One day, Sam came home extremely upset. She and Ruby had argued, and when Samantha spoke with Mr. Monrow, he'd told her to stop being friends with Ruby and added, "Ruby doesn't like you; she talks about you behind your back."

"Sam, that doesn't make sense; Mr. Monrow would never tell you that Ruby talks about you. You must have misunderstood," I stated, shaking my head. Samantha could be dramatic! However, in the following weeks, Samantha continued to relay conversations with Mr. Monrow that were inappropriate. Every time Sam told me something, I told her she was overreacting and misquoting his words—until the day Sammy came home in tears. "Ruby hates me! Mr. Monrow told her I said mean things about her. Now she hates me! I don't want to see him anymore. You can't make me! I won't." She sobbed.

What in the world is going on? I wondered, noting the problems had begun *after* the pencil incident. *Why was the school counsellor acting as a fellow student and getting involved in issues between the girls?* The next morning, I angrily contacted Mr. Monrow to discuss Samantha's worries. He was dismissive and told me Samantha was making drama.

Sam could be a brat, sometimes difficult, headstrong, bossy, and dramatic. However, I got the sense Mr. Monrow wasn't being impartial. Still, I hoped to repair the relationship between Mr. Monrow and Sam. Both Mike and I felt it was important for Samantha to continue counselling. So, Mike and I made an appointment to meet with Mr. Monrow and the school principal.

The meeting was a disaster. It became obvious Mr. Monrow should no longer work with her. He refused to admit his role in escalating the two girls' issues, denied inappropriately discussing conversations between the two, and remained fixated on his missing pencil.

"You have students in and out of your office all day. Is it possible that Sam might not have taken it? Could it have been another student?" I asked.

"No, it was her," he angrily replied.

"Even though you didn't actually see her steal it?" I pressed on.

"No, I didn't see her take it, but it was her," he said.

Furious, I answered, "I do not want you to have any further contact with Samantha; under any circumstance. You're not able to be impartial, and your obvious dislike for her is causing further problems," I angrily declared.

CHAPTER 9

Accidents Happen

A few months after our meeting with the school principal and Mr. Monrow, I received a frantic call while at work. Samantha had been injured in physed class. The students had been playing floor hockey, and a male peer hit her ankle with the stick.

"I'm so sorry, Mrs. Proulx, she's being taken to the hospital by ambulance."

I thanked her for calling me and reassured her there was nothing to be sorry about. Sports sometimes lead to accidents. I envisioned Sammy reaching for the puck and colliding with a student whose stick flung across her ankle.

Quickly, I gathered my things and drove to the hospital. When I arrived, Sam was in a wheelchair on her way for an x-ray to confirm a possible fracture. Afterwards, I sat with Sam as the doctor put a cast on her ankle and foot. It would be six weeks before the cast would come off.

Sam was upset about having to miss dance for the time it would take her to heal. So, I drove her for ice cream, bought her a Disney movie to watch, and tried to cheer her up.

"Did you at least score?" I jokingly asked.

"No, I wasn't playing," she replied.

Confused, I looked at her. "How did you get hit with the stick if you weren't playing?"

It turned out Sam was on a break, sitting against the wall with a friend, waiting for the change in play. A male student had taken a stick, rushed at Samantha, raised it above his head, and struck her three times before the teacher took the stick away from him.

I was furious! It certainly wasn't the version of events I'd been told when called. *This wasn't a sports accident; it was an attack.*

The next morning, I marched into the school on a mission. "Why did the school tell me Sam had an accident while playing floor hockey?" I demanded.

Mrs. Andrews quickly explained that, the person who called me didn't know what had happened, only that Sam was injured in physed. The male student had extreme anger control issues, severe difficulties with comprehension, attachment, impulse control, and various physical problems.

Once I calmed down, my frustration with the school eased, but I still wanted to speak with the boy's mother. I dialed her number. His grandmother answered and immediately became upset when I told her what I was calling about.

"What do you want me to do about it? He's a little asshole. I can't control him. He's always in shit for something." I was taken aback. "His mother dumped him here, and now I'm stuck looking after him, and he's just as much trouble as she was," she added.

The way she spoke of him was troubling. Initially, I'd wanted some form of assurance he'd been punished and was learning consequences. *He attacked her with a stick!* However, after speaking with his grandma, I felt sad for him.

Later on, I learned the boy had FASD (Fetal Alcohol Spectrum Disorder). It's a disability caused by injury to the brain in utero. FASD can cause mild to severe injury, and no two individuals are exactly alike. The boy was severely affected. He had a full-time aide who was not supposed to leave his side at any time. However, the aid had stepped away for a moment. Hence, Sam's broken ankle.

I don't blame the school, although, at the time, I really wanted to blame someone. They did their best; they employed individuals who genuinely cared about the students from the gifted to the developmentally or physically delayed. They tried to promote an environment of inclusiveness. In many ways, it was the right environment for Samantha, even though some awful things happened while she was there.

CHAPTER 10

Hand In Hand

Samantha's final year in elementary was blissfully uneventful compared to previous years. The yo-yo effect of good and bad years was again on the good side. In retrospect, I now realize Sam was starting to deteriorate emotionally. She went from being friends with most of the class to a smaller group of children, some of which had questionable backgrounds. That was the year Sam first became interested in social media, and we allowed her to join Nexopia, Canada's first social media network designed for teens.

"Everyone is on it, Mom!"

The computer was in the living room, so what harm could an hour after school do? Later in the year, the mother of Sam's friend, Billie, gleefully told me that Billie had given Sam a stern lesson on the platform. It was then I realized—though common knowledge now—social media is a breeding ground for predators!

Sammy had developed a friendship with a "boy" who wanted to meet her. But the truth was that Billie was pretending to be the "boy." Billie took it upon herself to show Sam how dangerous talking to strangers could be and had been speaking to Sam for weeks without my knowledge. I felt Billie's mother showed a great lack of common sense. Her open amusement at the prank angered me, so I told her I should have been notified immediately.

Billie was often unkempt, her hair was usually tangled, her hygiene questionable. However, kids get messy when they're playing, so I didn't give it much thought. She was friendly, well-mannered, and I thought she was nice.

A few weeks after my conversation with Billie's mom, Sammy had a slumber party. The following morning, Billie's parents didn't show up to collect her. I spent the day trying to reach them by phone without success. By evening, Billie was still at our home. When I finally reached her mother, she told me she couldn't pick Billie up, so I ended up driving her home; her mom waved from the window as Billie ran to the house.

Another time, Sam spent the night there and went on the bus with Billie after school. The next morning, I went to collect her. Billie opened the door, and I walked into utter chaos. There were dirty dishes piled in the sink, across the counters, and over the kitchen table. A mountain of clothes and garbage was scattered against the walls and across the dirty floors. A narrow path between boxes and piled-up toys led to the living room, where a toddler sat in a diaper chewing on a filthy rag. The smell of urine made my eyes water. I quickly gathered Sam and left. The home made me feel anxious. Sam, however, seemed perfectly comfortable there. It was surprising because Sammy was a neat freak; she always liked things in their proper place—it gives her comfort.

Shayna came into our lives when Sammy met her at a youth group meeting that Sam attended every week. She loved going; it was an opportunity to meet local children, work on crafts, sing songs, and learn about God. Through the group, Sam made friends with several girls from the neighbouring communities.

Soon, Sammy was inviting friends from youth group for sleepovers and playdates. Shayna Sloan was one of those girls. Rather quickly, she and Sam became inseparable, although the girls went to different elementary schools.

Shayna lived with her father, Marvin, and two younger sisters. They lived in a small home on the east side of town. Since we lived in the country, I'd occasionally allow Sam to stay in town and visit Shayna after school while Shayna babysat her siblings until her dad got home. One Friday afternoon, I picked up Sammy from Shayna's house, and she sheepishly slinked out with short, choppy hair. She and Shayna had decided to cut each other's hair! It was horrific. They each put their long locks in ponytails and chopped away. Sam's hair was cut so close to her scalp. I was afraid it wasn't fixable. Shayna's was also cut close, but there was enough left to work with. Quite upset with both girls, I demanded to know why they'd done it.

Their response was: "It seemed like a good idea." Both girls were impulsive and mischievous.

The next morning, I called every salon in town, desperate to have someone fix what was left of Sam's hair and grateful for the weekend. I knew she'd get harassed if allowed to go to school with such a mess for hair. The hairdresser ended up shaving the back; it was the only option. Sam cried. She didn't need to be punished—her hair was punishment enough. However, I started restricting the amount of time she could visit with Shayna while Marvin wasn't home.

Keeping the girls away from each other proved to be a battle. They always wanted to be together, having quickly become best friends. So, we allowed Shayna to visit more often, and soon enough, she was a regular fixture at the house. Since Marvin was busy trying to raise three children independently,

I did most of the pick-up and drop-off of Shayna. It was far easier for me to jump in the car and pick her up than it was to ask him to load up his three kids to drop Shayna off at our home. I didn't mind. I was thrilled Sam found someone to connect with.

CHAPTER 11

The Future's Bright

The big transition from elementary to junior high is exciting, although a somewhat scary time. Both Sammy and Shayna were thrilled. They were finally going to be attending the same school! The junior high/high school was much larger than elementary, with an influx of children from neighbouring communities from grades seven to twelve.

In preparation, Mike and I met with school officials to discuss Sam's options. When I attended high school, there were two options, matriculation or the general diploma. However, for Sam, there were three possible paths, and it was vital to start thinking about the correct path for her. The first option was a regular curriculum, which would eventually lead to a diploma and all the possibilities for future education that a diploma provides. The second option was called knowledge and employability (K&E). K&E is a series of courses that start in grade eight, and it's geared towards a certificate. The program is geared towards preparing students for employment through

70

a more hands-on approach. It's more of a trades geared option. The third and final option was Life Skills.

The Life Skills program is exactly as it sounds. It is geared towards kids who need to learn personal responsibility and accountability. It helps individuals learn positive decision making, personal hygiene, and promotes psychological well-being. However, when presented to us, they said it was geared towards children with severe learning and developmental disabilities and focused on everyday skills.

After listing the three programs, they all recommended Samantha enroll in the Life Skills program. They felt Sam would never be capable of completing either of the other two options.

"What would she learn in Life Skills?" I asked.

"Well, the kids learn basic hygiene, a little math and reading, as well as skills in nutrition and health."

"Samantha doesn't need to learn about hygiene," I responded somewhat defensively.

They glanced at one another and nodded towards Mike and me, "Yes, we understand . . . but . . ."

"But she would never get a diploma?" I interjected.

"No. . ."

"Will she be able to get a job upon completing a Life Skills program?" I asked.

They met me with silence and looked around uneasily. Eventually, the school counsellor replied, "She should be able to do entry-level work."

"What does that mean? She's interested in cosmetology; is that an option?"

"No, she would need a certificate or a diploma . . ."

I glanced at Mike, took a deep breath, and responded, "Sam doesn't belong in the Life Skills program. I want her to get a diploma."

"Samantha will not be able to succeed in the regular curriculum," they answered.

"What about K&E?" I asked and once again heard how K&E was a certificate, not a diploma. I listened to their response and nodded thoughtfully. "But K&E leaves her with more options?"

The guidance counsellor looked earnestly at Mike and me and told us that because of Sam's unwillingness to access the additional resources available to her, Sam would not succeed in K&E. There had always been classroom aides available to help her during tests by either writing her responses or reading the questions, but Samantha refused the help. Instead, she preferred to muddle through on her own. I understood Sam's reluctance to access support. She wanted to be independent and worried about looking foolish to her peers.

"We'll talk to Sam and try and get her to ask for help, but she's not going into the Life Skills Program. She doesn't belong there. We want her to go into the K&E Program."

Reluctantly, the school agreed.

CHAPTER 12

Zero Tolerance

I was about to break for lunch when my office phone rang. It was Sam, and she was hysterical. I could barely understand what she was saying between her convulsive sobs. The only thing I knew for sure was that she needed me. So, I quickly gathered my belongings, told my boss—who immediately got annoyed—that I had an emergency, got into my car, and drove to the school. When I arrived, Sammy was waiting by the front doors, her arms protectively crossed against her chest. Her eyes were red and puffy, tears streaming down her face.

She ran to the car and jumped in. I pulled out of the schoolyard, drove around the block, and parked. It was her first day of junior high. I couldn't imagine what could have happened already. Sam had been so happy that morning, laughing and looking forward to a new year.

What she was telling me took me completely by surprise, and the harder she cried, the more difficulty she had catching her breath. I caught her words between wracking sobs. Her breathing came in short ragged spurts.

"I . . . uh . . . I . . . don't . . . uh . . . want to go to school anymore."

"What happened?" I anxiously asked.

"They're . . . they're calling me . . . a . . . a . . . lesbian," she cried.

"Who's calling you a lesbian?" I questioned.

"I went to my class, and . . . and when I got there, James . . . ugh . . . James started calling me a lesbian. Now, everyone is . . . is laughing and saying I'm a lesbian."

"Who is James?" I replied.

In a plaintive voice, Sam replied, "He's a guy in my class, and now everyone is calling me names! All . . . all the boys. I can't go back. Please . . ."

I tried to reach for her, but she recoiled. "I want to go home," she said. So, I sat quietly beside her until the tears slowly began to subside.

Once she was calmer, I wanted to know why James would call her a lesbian, but Sam said she didn't know. Over the summer, James had started a rumour which Sam believed to be over until she went to school. Shocked, I wondered why she hadn't told me about it before and gently asked her if she liked girls.

"No, Mom. I don't," she shrieked.

Eventually, I managed to convince her we needed to speak to the principal about the name-calling. Reluctantly, she agreed. I marched into the school past staring students, with Sam slowly trailing behind me. I was frustrated, my anger pulsating around us, moving us forwards.

Mr. Olsen, the junior high principal, sat across from us as Samantha described the mornings' events. "Why would they call you a lesbian?" he asked.

"I don't know," Sam whispered and started crying again.

Raising his eyebrows, Mr. Olsen suggested she ignore them. "I tried, but they won't stop," she cried.

He looked from Sam to me then told us he couldn't do much about it.

Angrily, I insisted the boys be punished. Somewhat reluctantly, he agreed to have a talk with them, which he did. Afterwards, the name-calling receded while inside the classroom, but breaks were another matter. They continued to taunt Sam, and it spread; soon, Ruby, Sam's once long-time friend, joined in the mix. The little girl who'd brought the plot to physically harm Sam to light in grade four was now a part of a new clique. Sammy was heartbroken by the betrayal.

I was angry and exhausted by the constant problems. Once more, I found myself regularly marching in the school for a chat with Mr. Olsen. He was less than helpful; he told me he'd spoken to the boys, and beyond that, his hands were tied. When I explained the bullying continued and was escalating, he said he couldn't control everything happening in the school. I was furious.

"I thought this school had a zero-tolerance policy on bullying," I demanded.

"Are there any witnesses?" he calmly asked.

"It's happening every day, so I'm sure there are, but no one is going to talk," I bitterly replied.

"I can't do anything without witnesses," he retorted.

"Why do schools claim zero tolerance when they can't do anything?" I grimly replied.

Samantha was being abused every day, and he was unwilling to intervene because it was no longer happening inside the classroom!

The name-calling and intimidation quickly started taking a heavy toll on Samantha. She dreaded lunch breaks and avoided kids she once thought of as friends. One day, I stopped in to pick up Sammy; as I walked down the junior high wing,

Ruby said hello. Her fake smile and eager face angered me immediately.

"Don't speak to me. I know what's going on—you torment Sam every day," I snapped.

I felt out of control. Common sense flew out the window, and I injected myself as Sam's protector. It was draining, constantly going to the office to discuss what was happening. I was sick of hearing they couldn't do anything about it. Even though I encouraged Sam to respond to her aggressors in kind, she wouldn't, so I did.

Later in the year, Mr. Olsen called me at work to schedule a meeting between two other parents and me. Sam and two other girls had gotten into a verbal fight. I walked into the meeting with a chip on my shoulder. Not once had he scheduled a discussion between myself and the parents of the teens bullying Sam, but now he called me in to discuss Sam's bad behaviour.

My mood was foul as I sat down. I listened to the complaints against Sam, heard Sam's version of events, then turned to Sammy and asked, "Did you say those things?"

"Ye . . . yes," Samantha stammered.

"Okay, you're grounded, and your phone is gone for two weeks. Now, if we're done here, I need to get back to work," I added testily.

Mr. Olsen stared at me in disbelief and told me he'd expected me to defend Samantha.

"Why?" I asked. "I know she's not an angel. Of course I don't want her to be mean to others, but I also want something done when Samantha is the one being picked on," I angrily retorted and stormed out the door. It made me irate to receive a call for a meeting because of Samantha's behavior because he never reached out when Samantha was the one suffering abuse.

CHAPTER 13

Odd Interest

The more stress Sammy felt about school, the more she depended on her friendship with Shayna. The two girls were similar in many ways, including their learning styles, and although Sam had other friends, Shayna was her closest.

I've always preferred having Samantha bring her friends over rather than having her spend time away from home, but as she was getting older, I resumed allowing her to go to Shayna's after school. The girls often walked from Shayna's house to the youth group, and it was handy to let her walk with Shayna rather than drive Sammy everywhere. I became rather comfortable with the Thursday evening arrangement.

After a while, I started noticing a man hanging around. This man, Steve, was Marvin's friend, and the two men got together for a couple of beers or a barbeque while the kids happily jumped on the trampoline. Once, I even stayed and had a beer with them as Sammy gathered her belonging to come home.

I've always been a suspicious, cautious person, especially when it comes to people interacting with my children, so I kept a close eye on Steve around Sam. Soon, I noticed he was around more and more frequently. Eventually, he seemed to be there every time I stopped to get Sammy. His company started to feel off. I didn't care for how he interacted with Sam, Shayna, and her two younger sisters. He was always amiable, but the hair on the back of my neck prickled around him. His interest in Sam bothered me. He was always asking me questions about her likes and dislikes.

On a couple of occasions when I pulled up, he was jumping on the trampoline catching the girls and making them laugh. It creeped me out! As I approached the trampoline, he immediately jumped down and walked towards me. Smiling, he complimented my skills as a mother for raising "such a sweet girl."

I'm a firm believer in listening to instincts, and my instincts were screaming, *I cannot trust this guy!* Mike and I decided to limit Samantha's time at Shayna's and encouraged Shayna to visit Sam at our place.

Sam was furious, especially when we stopped letting her spend the night there. She didn't understand the reason for the sudden switch in rules and felt we were unfair.

Soon, once a week or so, Sam angrily stormed off and slammed her door, and yelled, "You're so mean," or "I hate you." More often than not, it was me she hated; she knew I didn't want her spending time there, although she didn't understand why. She thought I was trying to keep her from having fun. They say girls often blame their mothers, which was certainly the case in our home. We had a volatile, yet loving relationship, but we clashed more and more as she grew. Months went by before Sam started to adjust to the new rules; by that time, Shayna was spending almost every weekend at our home.

One Friday evening, I took the girls to A&W and dropped them off while I went for groceries.

"I'll pick you guys up in an hour," I yelled as I pulled away. Sam and Shayna waved and went in for a burger. When I returned, Sam ran out of the A&W and hastily jumped into the car. She was in a frenzy.

"Drive, Mom. Let's go," she commanded.

Surprised, I refused to move and demanded to know what was going on. There always seemed to be something going on!

As the girls had been eating, Steve had walked in. He'd noticed them immediately, sauntered over, and took a seat. After making small talk, he started questioning Samantha. He wanted to know the reason she no longer visited Marvin's home.

"My mom doesn't let me," she responded.

Steve had then tried to cajole her into convincing me to let her visit. When Sam had further explained it wasn't possible, he had flown into a rage; pounding his fist on the table, he'd yelled, "Your mother can't keep you away from me. I will kill her if she tries."

His outburst scared both girls. They'd sat in fear, quietly waiting for him to leave. In anger, he'd abruptly stormed out. Upon my arrival, Sam had bolted towards the car, with Shayna trailing behind her.

"Drive Mom . . . drive. I don't want him to see you," she said through hysterical tears.

I was enraged. "Did he really say that?" I demanded from Shayna, who silently nodded in response. I knew I should be afraid, but I wasn't. I was furious!

"Where is he?" I roared. Sam and Shayna jumped with fright then hastily pointed in the direction he'd gone.

"When did he leave?" I demanded as I put the car in drive.

"Mommy, let's just go home," Sam shrieked. "Please . . . he said he'd kill you."

"Oh, someone's gonna die, but it's not me," I retorted.

I drove, feverishly searching for him, but he was gone. All the while, Sam was begging me to take her home. *No one is going to threaten me or go after my daughter*, I thought. Slowly, with each block, my anger lessened. Abruptly, I pulled over, looked at Sam's pale face and reached for her hand. Realizing I was frightening her, I said, "It's okay, honey. Let's go home."

CHAPTER 14

For A Little While

I was standing in the kitchen, washing the dishes, and watching my dogs play outside the kitchen window. Abruptly, Samantha and Shayna bounced up behind me. "Mom, can Shayna live with us?" Sam asked.

Laughing, I shook my head and said, "No . . . I don't think her dad would like that." *Crazy girls.*

As I went back to the dishes, Sam went into several reasons why Shayna should move in. I smiled and shook my head; they were always coming up with crazy schemes.

"It doesn't work that way. Shayna can't move in. She has a home."

Dejected, the girls went back into Sam's room and cranked up the music.

Shayna and Sam got along exceptionally well, and in the time I'd known Shayna, I'd grown fond of her. She spent a great deal of time at our home having sleepovers, and we often took her camping with us. She was always polite, although somewhat reserved.

Over the next few weeks, Sam kept bringing up the subject of Shayna moving in with us, and I continued to explain the many reasons why that wasn't an option. Then, one evening, the phone rang. When I answered, Marvin's voice greeted me.

"So, I hear Shayna's gonna be staying with you," he said.

Laughing, I answered, "so I've been told."

"Does this weekend work for her to move in?" he replied.

I was taken aback—I'd assumed we were joking. I thought Marvin was making light of the situation, but he wasn't.

"Umm . . . what do you mean?" I cautiously probed.

"She doesn't have many things, so she should be ready. I'm happy to know she has somewhere to go," he responded.

It was a strange, surreal conversation. I'd known Marvin was having difficulty scheduling childcare, and I'd heard from the girls that he was taking more and more overnight hauls. One evening, I'd gone to his home to pick up Shayna for an overnight and ended up bringing one of Shayna's younger sisters along as well. The babysitter Marvin scheduled to watch the two youngest girls had taken the smallest to her house, but she sent her nephew, a male in his early twenties, to spend the night with the middle girl. It didn't feel right to leave a pre-teen girl alone overnight with the man, so I asked her to pack a bag and brought her home.

Unsure of how to respond, I found myself tongue-tied but eventually stammered my consent. Marvin claimed to need help for a month, and since Shayna was already a regular fixture, I agreed.

"Oh, um, sure. Shayna can stay here until you make better childcare arrangements. We're happy to help."

That weekend, Shayna moved in. She brought very few things, mostly clothes, and one family photo album. Within a couple of weeks, Samantha and Shayna had fallen into a routine. Shayna started calling us Mom and Dad, and both she and Sam began referring to themselves as sisters. I didn't discourage it. They were happy, and it was a temporary arrangement.

In the beginning, Marvin called once a week, but soon his calls tapered off, and what was meant to be a month turned into two. I kept encouraging Shayna to call her dad and visit her siblings, but she seemed disinterested. I should have questioned it more closely, but I didn't. Instead, I chalked it up to the excitement of having a long-term sleepover.

Soon it was summer, and we started spending a lot of time at the lake. We had a seasonal site, so we drove up every weekend. The kids had a great time. Karl usually brought friends, and Sam had Shayna. They were always water skiing, kneeboarding, and biking around the campground.

Marvin sent us a couple hundred dollars the first two months, but after that, he stopped contributing to her expenses and told us he couldn't take Shayna back "just yet."

Unsure of what to do, when we took Sammy shopping for school supplies and clothing before going into grade eight, we bought the same for Shayna. Even though it was a temporary arrangement, we treated her as part of the family. I was determined to not make her feel any different than Karl or Sam.

Shayna was a friendly, sweet and happy girl, but I often wondered how she adapted so rapidly to her new home, and I found her lack of interest in contacting her family concerning. She didn't talk much about them and only reached out when I insisted.

In September when the girls started school, I met with the school counsellor and transitioned Shayna from the Life Skills program into K&E with Samantha. I felt they had similar learning styles and was concerned about Shayna's future prospects if she continued in the Life Skills program. Reluctantly, the school agreed.

Within a short month, the school counsellor contacted me to report how pleased she was with how well the girls were doing. She said both girls were keeping up with their core subjects and loving their cooking and beauty classes.

That fall, when Sammy started up with dance classes, I asked Shayna if she was interested in enrolling in some type of after-school activity. The look of surprise on her face warmed my heart. I told her she could take anything she wanted. With tears in her eyes, she quickly chose drum lessons. Sam was also interested in drums, so both girls were enrolled. Without meaning to, I'd grown to love Shayna and accepted her as my second daughter.

Time continued on, and Shayna remained with us. I found myself including her in everything and becoming increasingly protective of her. I was angry with her father for his lack of contact.

After Shayna had been with us for about a year, we got a phone call with the horrible news that Marvin had been in a trucking accident and was in the hospital. Mike and I rushed a distraught Shayna into the intensive care unit (ICU) to see him. When we got to the hospital, four strangers greeted us—Shayna's aunts and uncles. I was surprised to learn Shayna had an extended family. Mike and I had wrongly assumed Marvin was on his own.

One aunt took Shayna inside to see her dad—Mike and I sat in the waiting room while the others fussed over us.

"We are so grateful to both of you for looking after Shayna. We wondered where she was staying," they said while excitedly pumping our hands. "We need to do something for the two of you; perhaps we can take you out for dinner?"

I found it strange and wondered where Shayna's family lived. *They must be from far away.* I rationalized. *Otherwise, why hadn't they reached out?*

"Do you need anything? What can we do to help you? Has Marvin been sending money for her expenses? Teenagers are expensive!"

Cautiously, I told them Marvin hadn't sent money in quite some time but explained that we didn't need anything. They continued to flit about expressing their gratitude.

"Ohh, well, that's not right. Please let us help you. Here is our phone number. Anything you need, just ask. Do you need some money? It must be so difficult; we know how trying Shayna can be!"

Somewhat defensively, I replied, "Shayna has been wonderful." Then, I changed the subject by asking them where they lived.

Quickly we learned the family was from our own community, and they all still lived in the area. Shayna's younger siblings were staying with Marvin's parents, who lived on a farm west of town. I was shocked! With so many family members in the area, why hadn't anyone called her?

As we continued to wait for Shayna, the aunt told us Marvin and his wife had been separated for some time. Initially, the children had lived with their mother, but one day she had dropped the children off and gone shopping. She'd never picked them back up. It broke my heart. *How could a mother do that? Those poor babies had been through so much!*

That evening, I asked Shayna about her family. She became quite agitated. "I don't see my mom, and I don't like my family. They hate me!" So, I didn't push the issue. I wanted her to feel secure and accepted. Not wanting to put additional stress on her, I hoped and figured if she needed to talk, she would when she was ready.

Marvin was in the hospital for several months. During that time, we drove Shayna to see him on various occasions. He had a severe brain injury, and the prognosis was poor. At best, he'd regain some of his motor skills, but he would never drive a truck again. It was going to be a long, difficult road. The likelihood of him being able to look after his children was very low. We settled into the knowledge that we'd be keeping Shayna with us indefinitely.

I continued to encourage Shayna to reconnect with her family while also reassuring her of our commitment to her, but I wanted her to have a relationship with them, especially her siblings. Eventually, she agreed to visit her sisters at her grandma and grandpa's. It didn't go well; she returned angry, crying that her grandpa had yelled at her when her younger sister went into the barn without permission. "You are supposed to be watching her," he said. "You're so irresponsible, and she is going to get hurt!"

That fall, school started up again, and we found it challenging to cover all the expenses of school supplies, new clothing, and busing fees. Shayna's aunt had called to offer help a few weeks earlier, so I decided to reach out. Shyly, I asked if their offer to help was still available and would they be willing to contribute towards Shayna's school fees. Her reaction was immediate, "We can't help with money; have you contacted family services?" she asked. Embarrassed, I thanked her for the suggestion. It was demeaning, and I felt foolish. When I did contact family services, they offered to send us eighty dollars a month. I was ecstatic. Mike and I decided to use the money to cover the cost of Shayna's weekly drum lessons.

A month later out of the blue, Shayna's grandpa stopped in at my work and handed me a cheque for two thousand dollars. "To help with Shayna's expenses," he said and walked away. It was the only time I ever met him. That same year, Shayna went to her grandparent's home for Christmas dinner. She was with them for a couple of hours when she called me in tears, begging me to pick her up. She had gotten into a fight with her cousin, and the family was angry with her. "They all hate me," she cried.

After some time, the two younger children went into foster care. Family services reached out to us to ask if we'd take them in, but our home was too small, and we couldn't afford two more kids, so we declined.

CHAPTER 15

Boys, Boys, Boys

It's tough being a teenage girl! All the insecurities girls feel suddenly become tenfold when hormones come into the mix. I know—I've been there and remember the angst of wanting a boy to like me, the neverending need to be accepted by my peers, and the overwhelming desire to be cool. It still makes me shudder when I recall many bad decisions I made in the name of peer approval!

Fortunately, I spent my teen years in a tiny community with girls I'd known since elementary. We were a close-knit group of girlfriends who always had each other's backs. We shared our dreams, our fears, and above all else, we protected one another! The idea of letting a friend go off with a stranger was unfathomable. We watched out for one another, and if necessary, bluntly told each other to get it together when one of us was behaving stupidly.

I wanted Samantha and Shayna to have the same type of bond I'd experienced as a teen. The girls referred to one another as sisters, so I fervently hoped they'd protect and support each other. Once the girls developed what I can only describe as *boy insanity*, that wish was especially important.

Sam had always been overly interested in boys, but now the two girls were obsessed. Every conversation was about a boy. Their appearance preoccupied them—makeup, hair products, and clothing were suddenly essential. They both wanted to date, although we told them they were too young. On a daily basis, they discussed getting their own cell phones. With Karl, we waited until his sixteen birthday to get him a cell phone, but we caved to the girls long before. They used those cell phones to check in with us, communicate with girlfriends, and have steady contact with boys.

It wasn't long before I was rethinking our decision. Both girls were always texting someone, but I didn't think there was any real harm until Samantha started sexting. A boy she liked began requesting inappropriate pictures. At first, she refused, but eventually, she gave in. He sent her a nude photo, so she reciprocated with the same. Within a couple of hours, she was a hot topic. The boy had forwarded the picture to various male classmates!

When Samantha came to me in tears, my immediate reaction was anger. I couldn't understand why she would send anyone a naked picture.

"Why would you do something so stupid?" I yelled.

The idea of sending a nude to someone would have never occurred to me. I was raised in a French Canadian community that never really accepted my widowed Mexican mother. So I was always determined to give zero cause to the lack of expectations for my sister and me. No one was ever going to look at me and think they'd been right all along. I would not disgrace my mother.

I was furious with Sam for sending the image and at the boy for distributing it. She claimed to believe he would delete the picture. This further infuriated me. *How could she trust someone so implicitly?* I reacted badly, and my anger brought on more tears, followed by a complete shutdown. Since a little girl, she'd always responded by withdrawing when upset. So when she ran to her room, slammed her door, and refused to speak with me, I wasn't surprised. My behaviour was instinctual. I didn't take into account how desperately she wanted others to like her.

The next week at school was traumatic. The same boys who used to call her a lesbian were now calling her a tramp. Once again, the hallways were a place of ridicule for Samantha.

I went to the school and demanded staff do something, but they said it was out of their hands. Sam had sent the picture willingly, and she would need to live with the consequences. In an effort to appease me, they said, "The teasing will eventually die down."

Sammy had made a terrible mistake, one that many girls make. Sexting is actually quite common among teens, and all too often, it comes with similar results. In Sammy's situation, neither the boys or the kids involved received any discipline. However, Sam got a bad reputation and another reason for torment. Today, passing naked images of someone without their consent is considered a criminal offence, but at the time, she was the one held fully responsible, not the boy.

As Internet popularity increased, the girls began spending more time on social media. At first, it was a teenage platform called Nexopia, and eventually, it was Facebook. It wasn't until much later that I realized how dangerous social media platforms could be to youth. It's a breeding ground for predators. They use the Internet to find vulnerable prey in the guise of friendship.

The girls started getting friend requests from strangers all over the world. Some people claimed to be teens, while others boldly admitted being adults. Neither girl was troubled by the friend requests, and I didn't discover what was happening for several months. Social media gives people a false sense of anonymity, and when it was new, I thought of it as a fun way to connect, which it is. However, people can use it for awful things.

Sam's bullying increased with the introduction of a cell phone and social media. The feeling of anonymity emboldened her tormentors. They were able to torment her on the school bus, at school, on the Internet, and through text messages. Sammy, however, appeared happy; she smiled, laughed, and joked around. So wrongly, I assumed the bullying was tapering off. It wasn't; it was just getting started.

Samantha and Shayna did everything together; they shared a room, were in the same grade, took the same electives, and attended drum lessons together. They were inseparable. This gave me a false sense of peace. I knew how easily Samantha could be manipulated, but I was less worried because Sammy and Shayna had each other. I thought one of them would tell me if they were having problems with school or other peers. Naively, I thought they were watching out for one another.

Sammy always wore her heart on her sleeve, and as the bullying increased, so did her posts showing her vulnerability. She was always complimenting other girls while hoping for validation and acceptance. When sad, she shared her feelings; when angry, she expressed her frustration. Both she and Shayna started posting provocative and scantily dressed pictures, which were quickly brought to my attention.

I started monitoring their Facebook posts and discovered inappropriate messages from strangers on both their pages. One by one, I blocked people and changed security measures while making the girls promise to notify me of strange friend requests. The girls were surprised by my reaction. They thought there wasn't anything to worry about and felt I was being overprotective.

"It's not like we'll ever meet them," they both said.

"It doesn't matter. What kind of man would want to be friends with a child? I don't want you girls talking to weirdos."

CHAPTER 16

Help

I got the call about Samantha's school suspension while at work. It was a beautiful sunny day, and the staff had found Sam smoking during lunch break.

"She was caught with *the smokers*. They gather behind the school. Smoking is prohibited on school property," the principal announced.

My first thought was a conversation I'd overheard between Sam and Shayna as we drove past a group of boys I'd never seen before, puffing away behind the school. The girls had been discussing Sam's crush on a boy. Shayna had been teasing Sam because he had two missing front teeth.

"Why doesn't he have front teeth?" I asked.

Unconcerned, Sam responded, "They got knocked out when he was younger."

"Why doesn't he get them fixed?" I asked.

Both girls shrugged their shoulders. "I don't think he lives with his parents," Sam replied and went back to talking with Shayna.

I sighed and told the principal I was on my way to pick up Samantha. When we got home, she was in a foul mood. After handing over her cell phone, she stomped out of the kitchen and angrily slammed her bedroom door. "I hate you," she screamed. *These I hate you outbursts are becoming a regular thing*, I silently noted.

Later in the evening, we discussed the suspension; Sam was ambivalent.

"Whatever!" she said.

I wanted to know when she'd started smoking. Was it a new habit born from her desire to impress the boy she liked? She refused to discuss it.

The next day, although Sam was home brooding, I went to work. Just after lunch, Shayna called.

"Mom, I don't feel good," she whimpered.

Her voice was strangled, coming in short bursts. Once more, I left work in a rush after explaining the situation to my angered employer.

When I picked her up, I immediately noticed her glazed eyes, coupled with ragged breath
and slight tremors.

"What did you take?" I demanded.

After a lot of prodding, Shayna reluctantly admitted to smoking pot with a boy named Marshall and Mrs. Lens. Mrs. Lens was the mother of a girl in Sam and Shayna's class. I'd known the girl when Sam was in kindergarten with her, but I hadn't known she now attended the same junior high as the girls.

Apparently while on lunch break, Shayna had jumped in Mrs. Len's car, and the three of them had driven around town smoking pot, after which they'd dropped Shayna off, and she'd gone back to class.

I was furious; I couldn't fathom how a mother would share drugs with teenagers. Shayna was shaking in my front seat. I worried the pot may have been laced with something, so I took her to the hospital. Her face was flushed, and she was crying uncontrollably. "I smoke pot all the time, I always have, and I've never felt like this before," she confessed. This information entirely blindsided me; I hadn't suspected a thing.

I sat beside Shayna in the hospital while the doctors monitored her, and after a few hours, they sent us home. Shayna went straight to bed to sleep off the remaining high. I sat up, pondering my next move. *Should I be contacting Mrs. Lens? It would surely lead to a confrontation, but would it make a difference?* After much thought, I decided not to contact her. I didn't think it would help.

We grounded both girls, and I hoped they'd learned their lesson. So, once the grounding period ended, we allowed them out again. While home, Sam and Shayna had been contrite, and for a little while, it looked like they were back on track. However, behind my back, they were hanging out with a group of kids who were regularly in trouble.

The girls lost interest in the youth group they'd once loved and started hanging out at a youth centre on the east side of town. It was a safe space for kids, opened by church leaders and designed to keep teens out of trouble. The place was busy; there were always dozens of teens mulling about when I picked up the girls, so we allowed it. *If it keeps them out of trouble!*

I pulled up in front of the centre and sat to wait for the girls. As the crowd of youth began to disperse, I called Sam, then Shayna. Neither girl answered their phone. Then, I texted both of them. They didn't text back. So, I sat back and waited while continuing to call them. Neither girl responded, although I kept trying. Once the place went dark and all the youth were gone, I pulled out of the parking lot and slowly made my way around town, searching for them. An hour later, I pulled back in front of the centre and again sat to wait.

Where can they be? Are they okay? The longer I sat, the more I waffled between worry and anger.

Finally, as I put the car in drive and began to pull away, I spotted them. The girls were surrounded by a pack of teens. Both girls were laughing and joking until they saw me. Abruptly they went silent and waved to their friends. Anxiously, they sprinted towards my car and jumped in the back seat. None of the teenagers came to the vehicle to introduce themselves. They simply slunk back into the darkness. Animated laughter lingered as they left.

Once the girls were in the car, I angrily jerked away from the curb. The fifteen-minute drive to our home was a mixture of tears and angry words. The girls begged for forgiveness as they handed over their cell phones. "You won't be needing these for the next while. You don't answer them anyway!" I yelled.

Over the next few days, the girls repeatedly apologized, and when that didn't work, they took to Facebook. Their pages were covered in "Sorry, Mommy" posts. As days went by and we didn't ease up on the grounding, Sam resorted to begging on social media, and extended family members started replying to Sam's posts. Having everyone know our family drama was disconcerting!

The morning their grounding ended, I sat at the kitchen table and handed the girls their phones. "I hope you've both learned your lessons. You cannot lie to me and say you will be someplace if you're not going to be there. Got it?"

"Yes, Mom," they both replied and gave me a hug.

I was concerned about their behaviour, didn't know most of their new friends, and worried about the lying and cigarette and pot smoking. However, I also felt they were basically good kids simply rebelling and testing. *It's a phase that most kids go through. I was rebellious, but it worked itself out.*

The following months were a series of ups and downs. Samantha kept promising she wasn't smoking anymore, and Shayna said she wasn't getting high, but there were many times I caught them lying about other things, so I wasn't sure if I believed them. They were still hanging out with their new friends, and we didn't know most of them. They also started talking about wanting to go to parties and lost interest in school. Getting them to complete homework assignments was increasingly difficult.

Social media was also extremely concerning. Sam was always sharing too much information. If we had a fight, she was sad, angry, or happy, everyone on social media knew! Family members started commenting and calling me to criticize her for airing her dirty laundry all over the Internet.

"Man, I kinda wonder what is going to happen at school today. I hope I have a good day; yesterday was crappy," one of her posts read. The one below said, "I am not having a good day. I got into a big fight with my mom, and now she won't believe me. She never lets me do anything." After this post, she followed it with: "Man, I don't know what to do anymore. Should I just give up or not give up?"

Sam's constant need for approval and validation was a source of contention between us. She spent a great deal of time complimenting girlfriends and asking them to reciprocate. It made her come across as needy and showed her vulnerability, which created an opening for more bullying. Once, she posted a question asking people to comment if they'd be sad if she died. Some of the responses were less than kind, and others were downright cruel.

Teddy Munrow, her old elementary school counsellor, called me one afternoon and told me, "Samantha came to me and said she wants to kill herself. I know you don't want me counselling her, so I'm letting you know."

I hadn't known Mr. Monrow was working with the junior high school, and because of our past experiences with him, I didn't want him counselling her, so I thanked him and made arrangements to pick Sam up from school.

Help

Frightened, I called our local mental health clinic. They instructed me to bring Sam in to speak to the child therapist immediately, which I did. When we walked in, a waiting therapist met us. She was a large robust woman with enormous bosoms, unkept shoulder-length brown hair, and bulging jowls. She crouched in her chair, licked her index finger, and handed Sammy a risk assessment questionnaire. Once Sam completed the assessment, the therapist leaned back in her chair, squinted her eyes, and wrote unknown comments beside Sam's responses. She then asked to speak to Sammy in private, but I pleaded for permission to stay.

"I'm terribly worried, so if I could stay, I'd really appreciate it. Just this one time, please?"

After Sam said it was okay, the therapist leaned slightly forward in her chair, and rocking ever so slightly, began asking Samantha a series of questions.

"I hear you want to kill yourself. Can you tell me about that?"

Sam discussed some of her feelings of sadness and said she sometimes wished she wasn't born. As I listened, my heart ached.

The therapist then asked Sam how she planned to kill herself. When Samantha didn't respond, the therapist continued.

"Would you hang yourself?"

Sammy shrugged and said, "I don't know."

I sat in silence, overcome with dread and confusion. *What is happening?* I wondered.

Next, the therapist said, "Are you sure? If you were going to hang yourself, how would you do it?"

I was speechless! Sammy was fidgeting uncomfortably in her chair. Her eyes met mine, then she quickly turned away. I wondered if she was worried about the therapist or me.

"Where would you hang yourself?" the therapist continued.

"I don't know," Sammy stammered.

"What would you use?" The therapist prodded as I listened in bewilderment.

"Would you do it in your closet?"

Finally, Samantha nodded uncertainly.

"Would you use a rope or a belt?"

"Umm . . . I have a robe, and I could take the belt from it," Samantha replied.

I sat in fear, silently thinking. *Samantha doesn't have a closet, but there are so many places she could hang herself from now that they've mapped out a plan.* Still, I continued to sit while the therapist encouraged Sam to elaborate. An ingrained belief that experts know best, coupled with shock at what I was hearing, kept me silent.

When it was finally over, the therapist asked me to step into the hallway with her. She nodded sadly at me and promptly gave me her diagnosis. "Samantha is bipolar and needs to be institutionalized immediately." My mind was reeling.

"What do you mean *institutionalized*?"

"You need to leave here, and go straight to this hospital," she said as she handed me a card. "When you get to emergency, have them admit her for observation."

"Wh . . . what?" I stammered.

"She has a plan, and if you want to keep her safe, you have to follow my instructions," she replied.

Dear God, does Sammy really need to be institutionalized? I wondered.

Confused, I thanked her, and Sam and I left. Sam was silent on the way home, and I pondered what I'd witnessed. We *should* trust the professionals, but what I'd seen didn't seem professional. If Sam didn't have a plan before we got there, she certainly had one now! Had I not sat in the interview, I would have trusted the therapist's suggestion and taken Samantha to the hospital, but I didn't trust her. *Was she seriously telling me to have Sam committed? Would the hospital really admit her?*

She's the professional. No, she gave Sam a plan! What if she's right and Sam tries to kill herself? Oh, my God, what if she's right?
When we got home, I placed a hysterical phone call to our family physician. He came to the phone immediately, and I explained what had happened. He knew Samantha, had treated her most of her life, and was actively involved in her current care. I asked him for his thoughts on the situation.

"If I take her to the hospital, will they really do an immediate intake? She says Sam is bipolar. How can she know that in one hour?" I asked.

Sympathetically, he explained that the chances of an immediate intake were highly unlikely and kindly offered to see Sam the next day in his office.

The following morning, I took Sammy to see our physician, who spoke with her and made a small change to her anxiety medication. We discussed therapist referrals—I refused to take her back to the local mental health clinic. We also made plans for him to see her regularly until we could have a new therapist. He felt she was not in imminent danger but should be monitored.

A day later, I received a phone call from a child care service agent, who informed me a complaint had been filed against me by a concerned individual. The unknown individual said I was endangering my daughter's well-being. They needed to follow up on all complaints and would be doing an investigation.

I snapped, "You mean the mental health therapist called you."

"I can't disclose who filed the complaint."

Furious and in a raised voice, I replied, "That woman is a quack. I've taken my daughter to see our doctor, and she's not in immediate danger. I'm not ignoring the situation, just not following her advice. She's a danger to children and should have her license revoked because she doesn't know what she's doing. That woman is going to get some kid killed! So tell her to back off."

"Umm, again, I can't tell you who made the complaint," the worker responded.

I closed my eyes, took a slow deep breath, and lowering my voice, I forced myself to speak slowly and deliberately.

"I have taken Samantha to see our family doctor. You are welcome to contact him." Fortunately, the worker was understanding; she thanked me, said she'd contact our doctor, and hung up the phone.

CHAPTER 17

Murky Waters

Fifteen is a tough age. Teens at that age are not adults, but they're no longer children. It's often around this age that the desire to exert independence can lead to rebellion. I moved out when I was fifteen. My home life was chaotic, so I took a part-time job and moved in with my boyfriend (who later became my husband). Living away from my mom gave me the freedom I wanted and responsibilities I didn't expect. Once I moved out, I hung out with whomever I liked and lived life as I pleased. My mother could no longer dictate my choices. However, I was also completely focused on graduating from high school and working towards a better future. So while living away from my mother's home wasn't ideal, it wasn't detrimental.

At the age of fifteen, Samantha and Shayna wanted more independence, but they lacked maturity. They wanted to attend school parties, hang out with their friends, and make more decisions. Although they were childlike in many ways, we decided to give them some freedom and let them go to their first teenage party. It was on the outskirts of town, and *everyone* was going. It wasn't that I particularly relished the idea of them attending, but I also wasn't naïve enough to think they'd never go to a party.

The first time they went out, I picked them up at midnight without incident. A few months later, when they went to a second party, I picked them up, and Samantha helped Shayna along. When I parked, Sam guided Shayna into the back seat then quickly jumped in beside her. Both girls were unusually quiet as I pulled away. Striking up a conversation, I asked them about their evening. Shayna mumbled, then promptly fell asleep while Sam barked, "I don't want to talk about it."

When we pulled into the yard, Samantha stormed into the house. I shook Shayna half awake and helped her inside. Once in the door, she sluggishly stumbled to her bed and promptly fell back asleep. Sharply, I asked Samantha how much Shayna had to drink. When Sam didn't respond, I changed approaches and sat on the side of her bed.

"What happened?" I asked. In a burst of outrage, Sam told me Shayna had sex in a field where everyone could see her.

"Her and Wayne had sex in a field?" I stammered.

"No. Wayne wasn't at the party; it was someone else."

"Are you sure?"

"Yes, Mom! I'm sure. I saw her!" Sam hissed back.

Trying to make sense of the situation, I shook my head. "Are Shayna and Wayne still dating?"

"They were when we went to the party, but now he'll probably break up with her," she replied.

"Who was the boy Shayna was with? I thought she was a virgin? How did this happen? Was she hidden behind something? Did she know everyone could see her?" The questions tumbled from my mouth; I had difficulty understanding. Fear was starting to hit me.

"I saw her, Mom. Everyone saw her! I tried to get her to come with me, but she wouldn't. She was all over him. They just did it right there!"

Glancing towards Shayna, I took a step in her direction and shook her. "Shayna . . . Shayna, what happened tonight?" Shayna covered her face with the blanket, moaned, and turned over. Again I tried, but it was no use.

"She's drunk, Mom. She drank a whole bunch; she's not gonna wake up," Sam spat.

"What did she drink?" I questioned.

"I don't know. . . lots." Reluctantly, I admitted Sam was right and agreed to wait until the morning. It was a restless night; I was appalled and fearful. The next morning, after breakfast, I spoke with Shayna. At first, she denied everything. She said Sam was lying, but eventually, tears filled her eyes, and she admitted to being with a boy. Her memory was hazy; she wasn't sure if she'd had sex or not and claimed, "He tried, but I don't think we did it."

"How can you not be sure?" I asked.

I needed an explanation, but I was frightfully aware of the various ramifications. Sexual connotations are very different for girls and boys. Even now, boys are admired for their prowess, but girls are criticized and labelled. I've known many women who have found themselves in situations they couldn't control; it's confusing, frightening, and often embarrassing. So, I prodded for clarity. *Did she consent or not?*

Eventually, Shayna broke down. She said she had asked him to stop but didn't know if he had. She'd drank a lot, and her recollections were sporadic. My head was in turmoil. *Had she been raped? If someone can't make a conscious decision to engage in sexual intercourse, is it considered rape?*

As Shayna cried, I put my arms around her and tried to provide comfort. Once the crying began to subside, I cautiously asked if she was willing to report the incident to the police.

"Honey, you have to be sure. If you said no, you've been assaulted, but if you said yes, you have to admit it."

"I want to report it, but I don't know if it really happened," she said.

At the police station, while filing an official report, Shayna was withdrawn and confused. She whispered her recollection of events, then quietly wrote them down. Her hands shook as she answered the officer's questions. Once they took her statement, we went to the hospital, and they conducted a rape kit. As they collected the specimens, I silently held Shayna's hand.

"Mom, don't leave me," she whispered.

"I won't." *Why did we let them go to that stupid party? She looks so small and frail,* I thought.

Afterwards, I gathered our belongings. As I stepped outside the door while Shayna dressed, the police officer motioned me over and sadly confirmed her hymen was ruptured. There was no internal damage, so they weren't able to pinpoint if it happened the previous night or some other time.

"I'll be in touch," the officer said and squeezed my arm. "You can take her home; I assure you I'll find out what happened. I'm going to be questioning the boy and all the witnesses."

The following days were a whirlwind involving several phone calls with the officer, several doctor visits for Shayna, and an unspoken layer of hostility between Samantha and Shayna. Sam was angry. She said Shayna was lying.

"Shayna wasn't raped, Mom. She wanted to be there."

"Sammy, that's not what she says. We have to support her and be here for her," I replied, but in truth, I had reservations. However, I pushed my doubt aside because I was certain of one thing—Shayna needed my help. Whether she was assaulted or had made an accusation she felt unable to take back, she needed us. Either way, she was going to need our support and professional help.

When Shayna first came to live with us, she had no contact with her mother. For a long time, I hadn't even known her mother was around. One afternoon, after nearly a year of Shayna living with us, the phone rang. It was a woman claiming to be her mom. Shayna refused to take the call. Over the next few months, her mother kept reaching out.

Eventually, Shayna answered the phone. They'd had a brief conversation upon which Shayna hung up, ran to her room, and threw herself on her bed. I followed her in and asked if she was okay.

"She wants to see me. Do I have to go? I don't want to see her."

I'd told her she didn't have to do anything she wasn't comfortable with while also encouraging her to give it a chance. After several more calls, Shayna agreed to meet with her mother, and slowly, they began the long process of reconnecting.

Truthfully, I didn't particularly like Shayna's mother. She'd abandoned her children, had chosen her boyfriend over them, and hadn't bothered to contact Shayna until long after she'd been with us. I was protective of Shayna and felt called to look after her. In my mind, God had sent her to us, and I loved her as my own. Sometimes, I found myself picturing her future wedding, the same way I envisioned Karl and Sam's.

Shayna's mom was always pleasant on the phone, and I felt it was important to keep the lines of communication open to provide the best care possible for Shayna. A few weeks after Shayna's assault, her mother called me.

"You know Shayna lies, right? This isn't the first time she's made something like this up. I feel sorry for the poor boy," she said.

Her immediate defence for the boy bothered me. My heart ached for Shayna as I listened to her mother, and although I suspected Shayna wasn't truthful, her mom's tone was cold. It convinced me of Shayna's need for someone in her corner.

There were many things I didn't yet know about Shayna's childhood, but some horrors were coming to light. I was aware that her mother's boyfriend had been in prison for pedophilia and that her mom had chosen to believe his innocence. *How does a mom choose some guy over her own children?*

Shortly after the phone call with Shayna's mother, the officer investigating Shayna's assault contacted me. Because there wasn't enough evidence to pursue the matter, and although many kids had seen her in the field, no one knew for sure if it was consensual or not. So, the police had no choice but to drop the case.

"I'm sorry, Monika, but based on my investigation, I think she might have made the rape up. It could be that she feels ashamed or guilty."

I thanked him and hung up, feeling both sad and worried. Could I make Shayna go for therapy? What if she refused? What recourse did I have since I wasn't legally her guardian? We never made Shayna's living arrangements legal, and although I considered her my daughter, I didn't really have any rights.

CHAPTER 18

In A Blink

The day my children were born, I made a vow always to protect them, no matter what. I recall many conversations with my friend, Diana, discussing our fears about our kids' futures. There are so many unknowns; it can be overwhelming to think about the millions of things that could go wrong! In fake bravado, I'd express the lengths I'd be willing to go to if my child needed my protection, but it's hard to know what a person would do until the time comes.

After the events of Shayna's encounter, we kept a tighter rein on the girls, and I worked at convincing Shayna to attend counselling. She was extremely reluctant.

"I had counselling years ago, and it didn't help with anything," she cried. Unsure of how far I could push the issue, I gave her space but continued to advocate for therapy.

Shayna's boyfriend, Wayne, had initially been angry with her after the party, but soon after, he committed to be supportive. Wayne was a shy, withdrawn, lanky boy with lovely black curls and a quiet demeanour. He was always showering

Shayna with gifts and compliments. He was eager to please her; it was obvious how crazy he was about her.

Wayne was Shayna's boyfriend and Sam's friend. I liked him; he was polite and friendly, although somewhat self-conscious. Both Wayne and the girls lived on acreages, so Shayna didn't have much opportunity to see him outside of school. Occasionally, I allowed the girls to stay in town to watch football practice, but more often than not, it wasn't feasible. So, when Wayne's mom called me and asked if the girls could go to her home for a barbeque, I agreed to let Sam and Shayna visit. After the initial visit, we let them go there quite often. They attended his family get-togethers and spent many afternoons hanging out. I'd drive them there and pick them up after a few hours. His mother was a friendly, hard-working woman who always welcomed the girls with open arms.

One beautiful wintery Saturday afternoon, I dropped them off for a scheduled visit and made plans to return after supper. It was mid-November, and the sun was shining against the glistening snow. It was a picturesque winter day, but within a couple of hours, the wind picked up, and heavy snowflakes started blowing across the roads. Soon, there was a weather advisory.

I spent the day cleaning the house and going over Christmas lists. Around five o'clock, the phone rang, so I scrambled across the freshly washed floors and rushed to answer. Shayna's aunt's voice brought me to a halt. Curtly and briskly, she informed me she had Shayna.

"Why?" I responded, confused.

"We picked her up. She called and asked us to."

Shayna's aunt told me that Shayna and Samantha had a fight, after which Shayna had called her. My mind was reeling. They had never fought before, and I couldn't understand what would make them fight now or why neither girl had called me. The last time Shayna had spoken to her aunt, they'd had another argument, and Shayna told me she didn't want to see her again, so why would she call her now?

"I don't understand. What's going on? What did they fight about, and when did this happen?" Shayna's aunt said she didn't know the details, only that Shayna had punched Sam.

"Do you have Samantha?" I asked.

"No, she stayed at that boy's house." I shook my head to clear it. It didn't make sense; nothing was making sense.

"Can I talk to Shayna?" I asked.

"No," she abruptly replied and hung up before I could ask further questions.

Confused, I stared at the phone for a moment, then dialed Samantha. The phone repeatedly rang without an answer. Gazing out the window, I realized how poor the visibility was. *Why wasn't she picking up?* I wondered as I called again, pacing and waiting for her to answer, but it went to voicemail. Frustrated, I hung up and quickly redialed. Again it went to voicemail. My chest tightened with fear.

I didn't know Wayne's house number, so I called his mom's cell. She picked up on the third ring, sounding happy and relaxed. Anxiously, I asked to speak with Samantha. She listened quietly as I explained why I was calling then informed me she was in the city for the weekend. A sinking pit hit my stomach. The girls had lied to me! They'd said she would be at the house. *Who was supervising them?* Quickly I answered my question. *No one!*

After hanging up, I paced back and forth then once more tried to reach Samantha. Again, it went straight to voicemail. In desperation, I called Shayna's aunt. She wouldn't let me speak to Shayna, so I asked her if either girl had been hurt.

"Sam was bleeding, but she seemed okay."

"Bleeding? How badly, from where? What exactly happened?" I stammered.

"I don't know. Shayna won't talk about it, but Samantha looked fine when I left. This is your fault! Why would you let them go to that boy's house anyway?" she retorted.

What was happening? I felt I'd been punched in the stomach. Her words angered me, especially since I was asking the same question. When I replied, I was defensive. I told her she had no right to question my choices. She responded by accusing me of being irresponsible and placing Shayna at risk, then abruptly, the phone went dead.

Furious, I dialed Sam again. Finally, she answered. Her voice was low and raspy.

I asked her what happened and told her I was on my way to get her, but she said she didn't want me to come. I wanted to console her, but her refusal let me pick her up angered me.

"You are coming home," I spat.

Sam has always pushed me away when hurt or upset; her difficulty processing emotions often led to her storming off and refusing to communicate. It's been a source of friction between us all her life. I prefer to deal with emotions head-on, but she shuts down. Her refusal to talk usually escalated our arguments because of the push and pull between us. Years later, a psychologist expressed admiration for Sam's instinctual retreat. The psychologist explained Samantha's withdrawal was her way of processing difficult situations until she could self-regulate.

However, that evening, her need to cool off was the last thing on my mind. My teenage daughters were out of control, lying, drinking, and fighting! I needed to get to the bottom of the situation and find out what had happened. I was apprehensive. *How badly was Sam hurt?*

Samantha and I argued on the phone. She was rude, refused to come home, and said she wouldn't get in the car if I went to get her. She wanted to spend the night. I was livid!

Sam had always been headstrong but openly defiant, *never*! I didn't know how to proceed. If I had acted the way she was acting, my mother would have slapped me, and I would have slumped in defeat, but that wasn't something I felt prepared to do.

I kept arguing with her, demanding she listen, but my words fell on deaf ears. *Should I force her into the vehicle?* I wondered. When she hung up on me, I raked my arms across my dresser in irritation. Everything flew across the room; perfume, makeup, and knick-knacks scattered across the floor. A jewelry box hit the wall and left a large dent; the mess brought me to my senses. Having grown up in a household of minimal financial means, I'd never destroyed anything before. Everything we had was precious, to be cherished, but that day, I lost it.

Standing back up, I slowly started the task of picking up broken glass and rectifying the mess. The caged animal feeling subsided as quickly as it came. *What was I supposed to do now? She's coming home*, I thought, *but how do I make that happen?*

At that point, Karl and his girlfriend walked in the front door. He came to my room and asked me what was wrong. As quickly as the anger had subsided, it reared its ugly head again. Crying, I screamed my frustration at him.

"I have to go and force her to come home," I said while reaching for my coat, "but she says she won't come."

"Mom, you can't drive while you're like this," he said. "The roads are terrible."

"She has to come home," I cried.

"We'll go get her," he answered and headed for the door.

"She won't come!"

"She will. She'll come with us," he replied as his girlfriend nodded.

Two hours later, I heard Karl drive back into the yard. Samantha was with him, although angry about having been picked up. Furious, she stormed down the stairs and slammed her bedroom door as I yelled, "We will talk about this in the morning, and you're grounded."

111

The next morning, when Samantha was willing to talk, she told me they'd all been drinking throughout the day. Shayna and Wayne kept disappearing to his bedroom. Bored and emboldened by alcohol, Sam had barged in. The two girls argued, and Samantha had called Shayna a hussy.

Furious, Shayna jumped from the bed and shoved Samantha back. Samantha stumbled and fell. Once down, Shayna repeatedly kicked her. Startled, Sam hadn't even tried to defend herself. Eventually, Wayne stepped in and forcibly pulled Shayna away from Samantha. Shayna had turned her uncontrollable rage towards him. She had slapped him, scratched, kicked, and sworn at him. Then abruptly, she'd stormed out to call her aunt.

As Samantha spoke, my mind reeled. I'd heard of Shayna's volatile temper, but we'd never experienced it. Not once in the two years she'd been with us. The girl Samantha described seemed unrecognizable. I recalled a conversation I'd had with Shayna when she'd first moved in—she'd told me about hitting her mother in a rage.

"That is behaviour we will never tolerate here," I'd replied. "We never hit each other, so that can't happen if you want to live here."

"I know. It won't," she'd said.

I'd meant every word at the time, but that was before she was my daughter. A parent doesn't throw their child away! *What am I supposed to do now?*

I called Shayna's aunt later that morning and asked to speak with Shayna. Again, she refused to come to the phone, which didn't surprise me. I assumed she was thinking about our conversation from long ago, the same way I was.

Figuring Shayna's aunt should know the details, I relayed Sam's story and said it would be best for Shayna to stay with them for a while. I needed time to figure things out.

A couple of hours later, I answered the phone to a hysterical Shayna, begging me to pick her up and take her home.

"Mom, please," she cried between ragged sobs. "They said they're going to send me to social services. I can't stay here." *Surely that can't be.* I thought. I remembered my mom threatening the same to me once. It had left a strong impression on me. So, I asked to speak with her aunt, who unfortunately confirmed Shayna's claim. They felt she was out of control, "having sex and drinking," and they couldn't possibly keep someone like her in their home.

They spoke of her like a rabid dog in need of being put down. I tried to reason with them and told them I just needed time, but they didn't care, so I told them I was on my way to get her.

Once in the car, I announced, "You can only come back if you agree to get counselling."

"Okay," Shayna replied, her head down, her eyes sad.

At home, the atmosphere was tense. The girls' relationship was fractured. They tiptoed around one another. Sam's weariness was palpable, and Shayna seemed subdued and unsure. I spent a great deal of time talking with the two of them, trying to find a way to begin the difficult task of rebuilding trust. Secretly, I wondered if they could ever restore the relationship and if I was making a terrible mistake by welcoming Shayna back, but she had nowhere else to go, and I couldn't turn my back on her. What kind of mother would I be if I did?

CHAPTER 19

Aloha

Our house became unusually quiet. Although Sam and Shayna still shared a room, they seemed to tiptoe around each other; conversation was a bare minimum. Christmas was quickly approaching, so I focused on family bonding activities, like decorating the house and tree. We had a Hawaiian vacation scheduled for early in the new year, and I planned to get Shayna into counselling when we returned. While keeping a watchful eye on both girls, I encouraged them to try and work things out. Sam seemed afraid of Shayna, but I didn't know what else to do other than take her back in.

With the Christmas music, hot chocolate, and tree decorating, the girls slowly started warming to each other, and I began to ease up a little. *Perhaps it would work out!* When the school shut down for Christmas break, we let the girls invite two friends for a slumber party. That Friday evening, Mike and I got home from work and immediately regretted our decision. The girls and their friends had gotten home after school and immediately broken into the liquor cabinet.

All four teenage girls were cackling in the living room, an empty mickey of vodka on the floor. It was a slap in the face. I'd been so stupid to trust them, and they'd only been home a little over an hour before me! Angrily, we sent them to their room. I felt at a loss! *Where was all the disrespect coming from?* That Christmas season was a nightmare. Both girls were in constant trouble. They were disrespectful and out of control. As I hung the stockings on Christmas eve, I told them I would be leaving theirs empty. Of course, I didn't do that. Instead, we grounded them off their phones and social media.

"There will be no contact with any friends throughout this holiday season!"

The next morning as we sat around the Christmas tree opening gifts, I felt weary. I was walking on eggshells, afraid some type of blowup would ensue in front of our invited guests.

January came and went. As our trip approached, the girls seemed to settle back into acceptable teenage behaviour. There were good and bad days, but the constant bombardment of rebellion eased. I hoped we were turning a corner.

Planning our Hawaiian vacation had been quite complicated. Gathering the necessary paperwork for a passport and the appropriate documentation giving us permission to travel with Shayna had taken months. We'd started the process long before the girls had their fight, but even after, we never considered not taking her.

The morning we headed to the airport, both girls were on cloud nine. They giggled excitedly. It was contagious. We all felt uplifted and eager to spend three weeks in the sun. At the airport, we met up with Mike's sister, her husband, and their two sons. It was going to be a vacation to remember!

We spent five days in O'ahu, visited Waikiki beach, and toured Pearl Harbour, then boarded a small plane for Maui, where we stayed for the remainder of the trip. The cultural differences broadened the girls' perspective, and the beaches cleansed our spirits.

Soon, the girls were laughing and connecting the way they use to. It warmed my heart, and I felt confident that once we returned home and both girls were in therapy, life would get back to normal.

One morning, we drove the Hana Highway, Maui's famous winding road with six hundred and twenty curves! Although the intention was only to go halfway as instructed, the day was so beautiful, so we decided to continued. It took us to majestic waterfalls and beaches that took our breath away. Along the road, we discovered a lonely old church sitting high on the rocks, so we stopped, took pictures of the girls and their cousins running about, then ate a snack before heading back to our hotel. By the end of the drive, Shayna was nauseous from all the turns in the road and the heat.

Once back in our room, Shayna had a cool shower, Sam curled up and watched television, and Mike and I relaxed with a drink. I was content; the girls were closer again. The sunbathing, whale watching, and luaus had worked their magic.

During our last evening there, we walked the Lahaina harbour. I took Samantha and Shayna for Henna tattoos, we ate at Bubba Gumps, and shopped for gifts. As we walked the pier, Shayna stopped at a small jewelry stand. Samantha and I were strolling slightly ahead, and Shayna ran up behind me, placed her arms around my shoulders, and said, "I love you, Mom," then she handed me a beaded necklace with tiny white shells. Happily, I put it around my neck. It was a perfect vacation. Life was good, light, and full of possibilities.

CHAPTER 20

Alone

We came home from our vacation refreshed. The girls went back to school, life had settled down, and everything was going well. A week after our return, I told Shayna I would start looking for a therapist for her, and she agreed. The next day, Shayna didn't come home on the bus.

I tried reaching her by phone, but she wouldn't pick up. *Where was she, and why didn't she come home?* Samantha said Shayna told her she'd be staying at a friend's for the night. I kept trying to reach her. Eventually, she answered and said she needed time to think.

Frustrated, I told her she couldn't come and go as she pleased. "You are only fifteen years old!" I stated.

The next morning, I drove to school, knocked on the classroom door, and asked to speak with her. When she came to the door, she avoided my gaze.

"I'm moving out! I want to be with my family," she stated.

I was stunned and saddened. I knew Shayna's family was all too happy to have her stay with us. So, I asked her who she was planning to live with. All the times I'd pushed her to repair her relationship with her extended family members kept rolling through my mind. I had shielded her from her their indifference—I'd protected her.

"I'm going to ask my grandma if I can stay with her."

"Your grandma? You've always said you hate your grandma," I answered in surprise.

Shayna shrugged, "Whatever."

Sadly, I replied, "You didn't have to run away. You could have told me, and I would have helped. We could've done this in a much easier way. You've always had the choice to stay or go," I said.

She shrugged, told me she didn't care, and stomped away. It was crushing. After nearly three years of living with us, she moved on as quickly as she had arrived.

I was hurt, not because she was leaving, but because of how she was doing it. I thought she made her decision in and effort to avoid counselling. *Why was she so afraid?* Looking back on our idyllic holiday, I realized she'd decided to leave before we'd even gone to Hawaii.

In the time she'd stayed with us, she had spent very little time with any of her biological family. She'd left her home and never looked back. Her ability to trust and love had been compromised at a young age. Unresolved traumas and feelings of abandonment hardened her. Through no fault of her own, she'd learned to survive by shielding her emotions. I hoped we'd been a safe haven for a little while.

After Shayna left, Sammy was angry. She felt betrayed and said she'd never speak to Shayna again. As the days went on, her anger turned to depression. She missed her sister. After spending every waking moment with Shayna, Sam was lonely.

She refused to talk to me and stormed off every time I tried to broach the subject of Shayna.

"I'm glad she's gone—she's a liar anyway," Sam spat.

To make matters worse, her bullies went into overdrive. It was as if they smelled her ripe emotions. While riding the school bus, the fellow students repeatedly victimized her. The incessant name-calling from the moment she boarded made the ride to school unbearable. They ridiculed her, called her a pedophile because her boyfriend was a year younger, and began calling her "Dirty Sanchez" because of her Mexican heritage. Quite quickly, Sam's boyfriend broke up with her and joined the pack of wolves rather than become a victim himself. Sammy was heartbroken. Within weeks, she'd lost her *sister* and her boyfriend. She felt the world was against her.

The pack mentality of her tormentors was frenzied. Every day was a nightmare of abuse. She wasn't safe anywhere. The ride to and from school kept her trapped as they circled. School hallways, classrooms, bathrooms, and even dance provided no respite. When she wasn't available, they reached out to her by social media and through her phone by text.

I was helpless to stop it; repeated visits to the school didn't help. When I approached the police, they wiped their hands of it, even when presented with copies of the social media harassment.

Within weeks, Samantha stopped wanting to attend dance lessons. The love she'd once felt for movement had been destroyed and replaced with apathy for life. Eager to keep some semblance of joy in Sam's life, I spoke with her dance instructor. I told her about the bullying Sam was experiencing, but her response was abrupt. "Well there isn't bullying happening in my class." She refused to speak with any of the students or even acknowledge Sam's plight.

Samantha's open vulnerability on social media continued to fuel her tormentors. Again, it created contention between us. I was monitoring her Facebook page and having her delete messages that aired her despair. She didn't understand how vulnerable she made herself. They labelled her as a fake attention seeker. Some peers posted demands for her to harm or even kill herself.

Our extended family wasn't supportive either. They criticized Samantha's inappropriate use of Facebook, and although I wanted her to stop posting as well, she wouldn't listen. Her heartache was eating at her, and her cognitive difficulties prevented her from understanding cause and effect.

One evening, while scrolling through Samantha's Facebook, I read a post where Sam expressed how sad she was. It infuriated me to see the vile things her peers replied. Insult upon insult followed her remarks. Those who tried to defend her faced a tirade of reasons why Sam should go ahead and end her life. I was appalled. *How can people be so cruel?*

In anger, I wrote a response under Samantha's post, "The kids who are bullying Sam, and yes, I do know who you are, need to back off. I will be contacting your parents."

The next day, I waited after dance class to speak with one of the mothers. Her daughter was a major instigator in Sam's school bus torment. She particularly relished the "Dirty Sanchez" innuendos and posted many messages on Samantha's Facebook page. The cruelty of her rants made my blood boil.

As I walked up to the mother, she informed me her daughter had warned her I'd be talking to her. "I don't get involved in teenage disagreements; the girls need to work it out on their own," she said.

"This isn't a teenage disagreement," I snapped.

As I explained the amount of bullying Sam was enduring, the mom was taken aback. "Allison wouldn't do that. She and Samantha used to be friends," she replied.

"I've read the texts and the Facebook posts," I answered. "Do you know what she's been calling Sam because of her Mexican heritage?"

She shook her head apprehensively.

"She calls her Dirty Sanchez— and I need it to stop—now!" I added.

I assume the mother spoke with her daughter as she said she would, but it didn't matter; Sam slumped into a deep void. The years of off-and-on abuse had taken their toll. She quit dance and hid in her room. It was heartbreaking to see her slowly deteriorating before my eyes. Her shutting down pattern was now the norm; I could barely get two words out of her.

Unsure of how to protect her, I began picking her up and dropping her off from school, and again I contacted the school for support, only to hear the usual. "There is nothing we can do."

It was infuriating! All the lip service to zero tolerance was just that. There were no consequences in place and no real plans to help a child in crisis. I was helpless to find a solution. Sam's constant debasement led to her slowly slipping away, and I was desperately trying to hold on.

CHAPTER 21

My Sister . . . My Friend

When Sam didn't come home, I panicked. I went to pick her up from school, but she wasn't there, and she wasn't answering my calls. She didn't want to go to school that morning, but I hadn't suspected she'd run away. Worried, I tried to reach her by phone. When she finally answered my calls, she bluntly informed me, "Shayna wants me to live with her at her grandma's, and I'm going to be staying there."

I was stunned. Just the night before, Sam had been furious with Shayna. Now, suddenly, she forgot her anger and planned on living with her. Sharply, I told her I was on my way to pick her up.

I drove to Shayna's grandmother's home and banged on the door. Abruptly, Shayna threw the door open and haughtily called Sam. When Samantha appeared, she didn't want to come home with me. I demanded she leave with me, and she vehemently refused.

Her defiance was infuriating. I had no rights where Shayna was concerned, but with Sam, I did, so although I knew she was struggling to deal with the constant bullying and grief over Shayna leaving, I couldn't allow her to leave home. It angered and frightened me that Shayna had even approached Sam with the idea! Samantha was already struggling with depression and withdrawing into herself. It was easy to manipulate Sam, and I felt Shayna was doing exactly that.

My fear manifested itself into anger; I was an outraged mother determined to force Samantha to follow the rules. Sam was equally determined, and a shouting match ensued. Promptly, Shayna's grandmother came to the door and intervened. She asked me to consider letting Samantha stay for one night.

"It will give you both a chance to cool down and talk it over in the morning," she reasonably declared.

I didn't want to go but reluctantly agreed. "I'll be back tomorrow!" I stated, glaring at Sam and Shayna.

Sam and Shayna had pushed me into a corner. Physically forcing Sam into the car would probably make matters worse and could even lead to a visit from family services, so I left. Once home, I wracked my brain. *What should I do?*

The next day was no better. Sam still didn't want to come home, but she had gone to school and was safe, so I gave in, with the understanding that I'd be picking her up regardless of her wishes on the following day.

When I drove up to get Samantha, she quietly got in the car, and we went home. "Mom, I miss my sister, and I want to live with her," she said. I understood the loss Sam felt. I, too, was finding it difficult to let Shayna go, but she had made her choice!

As I made dinner, Samantha went downstairs to her bedroom, gathered Shayna's belongings, and waited for Shayna to come to

123

her window and *steal* the items. Neither Mike nor I suspected the plan and were surprised when we spotted Shayna running around the yard with her arms full. Stray items slipped from her grasp and scattering behind her as she jumped into a waiting car. We didn't try to stop her. They were her things, although we had bought them. We had never intended to keep them from her but would have preferred her to knock on the front door.

I shook my head sadly as she drove away and fervently hoped all the sneaking around was over. Though I didn't have any anger towards her and even understood her reluctance to face us, I hoped that eventually, she would come to us. Shayna was free to live with her family, but I didn't want her to involve Sam. *Perhaps some distance would be good.* I thought. The next day, Samantha was gone again.

In the following days, family members shared their advice. "Let her stay with Shayna; it's a phase; she'll come home eventually."

I was horrified at the suggestions. *Sammy was acting out. How could we possibly walk away and hope for the best?* Instead, Mike and I launched into the offence. I argued, demanded, and sometimes resorted to pleading.

At first, Samantha was safely staying at Shayna's grandmothers, but soon enough, she stopped going to school, and both she and Shayna started squatting wherever they could. Eventually, in a desperate attempt to force Samantha into coming home, we began asking people to turn her away. At this point, we discovered several young girls in our community were running away from home and getting involved with the same *friends* Samantha and Shayna had.

Weeks would go by without any information on Sam's whereabouts, and I was obsessed with locating her. If I couldn't force her into returning, I would at least know where she was! Unable to concentrate on anything but Sam, I started spending my days searching for her. I neglected my business, fell behind on bills, and stopped talking to friends. The times I managed to track her down, we fought. What had once been rebellion was now pure hatred on her part.

When I wasn't searching for her, I was following her every movement on social media.

Her Facebook posts became more and more erratic! Her pictures were disturbing scenes of drunken stupors. She looked freakishly thin; her eyes were small black slits. The once bright humour and joy all but extinguished. I didn't know half the kids she was with.

One morning while scrolling through Samantha's Facebook account, I read a post designed to inflict pain. "I'm not a Proulx anymore. I'm now a Sloan like my sister."

Below her comment were several disappointed replies from family members telling her to stop disrespecting her parents. It was not only heartbreaking but also humiliating. Every day there was another post where Sam was bad-mouthing our family and airing her disdain for all to see.

While looking for any angle to get Sam home, I reached out to Wayne's mother. I'd seen him in some of Sammy's online pictures, so I thought she might know where Samantha was staying. However, when I called her, she informed me she had no idea where Wayne was. He had started using drugs and ran away from home. Much later on, I learned he'd been sleeping in the treehouse of another wayward teen.

Repeatedly throughout this time, there were small glimpses of light. Sometimes, Sam would turn up after a fight with Shayna or another unknown friend, and I'd dare to hope. On one such occasion, while Samantha was home, we spoke about Wayne. I'd heard a troubling story that Wayne had been beaten up at a party by Marshall (the teen who'd driven around town smoking pot with Shayna while she lived with us). When I asked Sam about it, she shrugged and coldly said, "Yeah, he owed Marshall some money. He should have paid."

"How can you say that? He's your friend." I was shocked. Then, I added, "I heard it was for ecstasy. Is that right?"

Again, she shrugged. She didn't even blink. I couldn't understand her lack of concern. She'd always been a fair, considerate, kind girl, and now, despite her friend's brutal beating, she didn't see anything wrong with it. Her lack of compassion frightened me.

That night, I rummaged through her phone while she slept and read through her text messages. One message from Shayna brought terror to my heart.

"I know how we can make some money and get our own apartment."

"How?" Sam replied.

"There's a guy who wants us to meet him in a hotel for a couple of hours."

"I don't know. I don't want to do that." Samantha texted back.

The conversation continued for several more messages where Shayna tried to convince Sam and then abruptly stopped.

My heart was pounding; I felt sick with terror. Reeling, I placed Samantha's phone back and tip-toed out of her room. *I had to get through to Sam before someone roped her into something unthinkable.* Frozen, I couldn't bring myself to talk about what I'd read. I didn't even tell Mike; doing so would have made my fears too real.

I never asked Samantha about the text because I knew with utter certainty that if she knew I'd taken her phone, she'd change her passwords, and it was imperative I have access to her phone and Facebook account in case she ran again, which she did a few days later.

Life was a rollercoaster ride. I never knew what each day was going to bring. When Sam was home, the first few days involved frightening displays of depression, but then she'd settle down, only to lash out and bolt again.

CHAPTER 22

Not Your Sammy Anymore

I purchased a hair salon six months before Samantha and Shayna started acting out. Eager for a change, I'd been looking at possible business ventures and leaped at the opportunity advertised in the local newspaper; also, both girls expressed an interest in beauty culture. I suppose I was also setting up future job prospects for the girls. Sam's original grade one psychological assessment was subconsciously in the back of my mind.

I didn't know the first thing about owning a salon, but the atmosphere was uplifting. Also, Jill, the previous owner, was friendly, eager to make the sale, yet keen to continue working. It seemed perfect. Jill said she loved her job but no longer wanted the responsibility of managing others.

Right from day one, there were difficulties. Jill was intense about how she did things and micromanaged every movement the other stylists made. She refused to stop answering the phone with "Howdy Pardner," balked at my desire to change the western décor, and disagreed with almost every comment I made.

At first, I tried to appease her. I supposed Jill was having a tough time adjusting to no longer being in charge, and since she was the main stylist, I wished to be considerate. However, soon we were in a silent battle. When I'd move a picture or rearrange a display, she'd move things back the moment I was out of sight. I tried to discuss my concerns, but she responded by leaving work for weeks on end.

"Jill, I can't have you gone all the time. You are the most experienced stylist, and the clients always ask for you."

"If I was going to work all the time, I wouldn't have sold," she said.

My stress over the girls combined with worry over the business increased daily. I was having difficulty staying focused. Sensing my unease, Jill swept in like a knight in shining armour and offered to become my partner. I knew a partnership would never work, but I didn't have the energy to disagree, so I told her I'd give it some thought. Next, she proposed buying the business back.

"Then you can focus on your girls!" she said.

We had several conversations about the logistics of transitioning ownership back, and I was seriously considering the offer. My head wasn't on work; my every thought was on Sam.

Then, behind my back, Jill started secret conversations with the other stylists in which she instructed them to report on my every move. I didn't have the strength to deal with her animosity, and because she had the most clients, I couldn't afford to let her go.

One Friday evening, after an especially tense work week, Jill stormed into my office and made an announcement. "I've decided not to buy the salon back from you. Instead, you need to walk away, and I'll help you by taking it off your hands.

Otherwise, I'll walk, and you won't have a senior stylist. You have until Monday to decide."

Tiredly, I nodded and forced a smile. Samantha had made a reappearance a few nights before, and I'd been making her come to work with me because I was afraid to leave her home alone.

"Umm, okay, we'll talk on Monday," I replied as she walked out the door.

Suddenly, Samantha walked in and asked, "Can I go to the dollar store?"

"I guess so, but don't be gone long. I'm almost ready to go home."

Sam walked down the hall, and after calming my shaking hands, I started the process of locking up. Once finished, I headed in the direction Sam had gone, but I couldn't find her. As I turned back towards the salon, I overheard yelling coming from the bathroom. Apprehensively, I approached the door and hesitantly pushed it open.

Two girls had Sam pressed against the far wall, pushing and screaming at her.

"What's going on?" I hollered as I forced the door open.

Immediately, I recognized the two girls. Both were frequent Facebook tormentors of Sams, so I quickly moved forward and shouted.

"I said what's going on in here?"

Startled, the girls backed up but kept yelling at Samantha. Angrily, I reached for Sam's hand and pulled her in my direction.

As we walked away, the girls pursued and shouted obscenities.

"You don't know what your daughter's done. She's a slut, and I'm going to kick her ass," one girl yelled.

It was nightmarish; these kids had zero fear! Still holding Sam's hand, I jerked around and faced the girls. "I don't care what Sam's done. Get out of here before I call the cops."

"She slept with my boyfriend, Marshall, and I'm going to get her," a stocky girl retorted.

My head pounded. *Sam slept with Marshall? Marshall the drugdealer? When? When did this happen?* I felt nauseous, so I took a long breath to settle my nerves and deliberately lowered my voice into a growl. "Did she force Marshall? I don't think so! You should be confronting your boyfriend instead of Samantha."

The girl stepped back as if slapped. Then, snarled, "I will." Abruptly, she turned to her friend, and the two of them stormed away.

As they reached the far door, she screeched, "Watch your back, Sam."

Shakily, I veered back towards Sam and hissed, "What in the world are you doing? Why would you sleep with that filthy boy?"

Sam didn't respond. She shrugged her shoulders as tears ran down her cheeks.

That weekend, unable to handle what felt like unflappable dread, I made a move to regain a little control in one area of my life. My father-in-law changed the locks on the salon doors, and Mike delivered a letter to Jill in which I fired her.

Disturbed by the knowledge of Sam's sexual activities, I decided to learn everything I could about Marshall. We discovered he was on a first name basis with the police, had been arrested several times for drugs, theft, and assault, and was facing a few court appearances. He appeared to be the ring leader, an intricate part of a pack of teenagers tearing across town. Other teens seemed to emulate him.

For some reason, girls found him appealing. He had many girlfriends and easily convinced them to run away to hang with him and his buddies. Oftentimes, girls as young as twelve fell into his crowd.

Marshall had favourite hangouts. His two favourites were homes on the opposite sides of town. A man in his mid-twenties rented the first one, and it was used as a party pad. Many kids often spent the night. The second was a run-down, dilapidated mobile home where a man lived with his infirm grandmother.

The number of teens running away in our community was astounding. Many parents feared for their daughter's safety, but the police were of little assistance. Sam was often disappearing for a week at a time. Then, she'd come back home. But usually, after about a week, she'd run again. When she was with us, she was always agitated and desperately anxious to speak with her friends. I wanted to take her phone and computer access away but knew if I did, she'd leave sooner, so I didn't. It was uncomfortable being afraid of my teenage daughter's reactions.

When she ran, reporting her as a runaway was of no use. The police couldn't get involved because she was fifteen, so I'd drive around for hours with hopes of catching a glimpse of her. Every time I ran into her, I'd pull over and talk to her. Her *friends* would protectively circle around her and glare. I could tell my constant interference was getting on their nerves. I could feel their animosity. It only served to encourage my commitment further. *Maybe if I anger them enough, they won't want her around.*

My tactic seemed to work. Sometimes, Sammy would come home, but she always ran again. Then, after months of the cat and mouse game, Sam came home visibly upset; her friends had kicked her out, annoyed because I was always tracking Sammy down. However, as usual, after about a week, they contacted her, and she'd ran back to them.

Once, I was outside, watering my flowers, and by the time I went back in, Sammy was gone. She had watched me from the window, packed a small bag, and walked down the dirt road to a waiting car. On my pillow was a note.

Dear Mom and Dad,

I am sorry for everything that has happened. I truly am, but I need to tell you something. I am not the same Sam at all. I have changed, and I'm sorry, but you need to let me go. Okay. I'm not your Sammy anymore!

The note was worse than the slamming doors or the fights. The unspoken pain in her letter terrified me! Shaking, a torrent of tears wracked my body. My heart was breaking! She said she wasn't my Sammy anymore, but somewhere deep within, Sammy existed, though trapped by something I didn't understand and couldn't control.

CHAPTER 23

Deep Waters

The pain was unbearable. Nothing brought me joy. I cared for only one thing—saving Sam! I hadn't seen her for almost a month. She'd gone underground; no matter where I drove, I didn't catch a glimpse of her.

Eventually, Sam called. Somehow, Marshall and his buddies had convinced Sam and Shayna that if they stayed gone long enough, family services would intervene and set them up with an apartment.

"Only *you* can come home," I snapped.

Detached and cold, Sam snarled, "I don't want to ever see you again."

After she hung up, I reached out to family services. I wanted to know if there was any truth to her claim. It didn't seem plausible, but nothing made sense anymore—the social worker who responded agreed to meet me at her office. Shayna's grandmother accompanied me to the meeting. Shayna had told her the same thing, and she, too, wondered if the girls could get their own apartment. However, she wasn't upset;

she thought I was melodramatic. "They are going through a phase and will eventually turn up," she calmly stated.

During the meeting, the worker explained there wasn't any truth to the girls' claim. They would not be setting them up with a place to live.

"Good . . . Samantha doesn't need to be further enabled. She needs to come home!" I reiterated.

Shortly after, I breathed a small sigh of relief when I heard the girls were once again staying at Shayna's grandmas. *At least I know where Sammy is,* I thought.

When I went by the house to see Samantha, I immediately noticed deep dark circles under her eyes. Her aloof and callous demeanour brought tears to my eyes. *Perhaps she truly wasn't my Sammy anymore.* As I spoke with Sam, a man peering through the curtains caught my eyes.

"Who is that guy?" I asked.

Sam shrugged and said he was a friend of Shayna's grandma.

"Why is he here?"

"I don't know. He stays here sometimes," Sam replied.

Her response made me uncomfortable. *Why was he staying there?* But Sam refused to discuss the matter further.

Samantha stayed there for a couple of weeks, and although I wanted her home, it gave me access to her, so I was grateful. However, the man was always there, even when Shayna's grandma wasn't, which worried me.

As it turned out, my apprehension was justified. He often found excuses to spend time with the girls and took an unhealthy interest in Sam. Once he tried to convince her to allow him to take pornographic pictures of her, and another time he broke into the bathroom while she was peeing.

Uncomfortable with his unwanted attention, Samantha left Shayna's grandmas, and I again couldn't locate her for over a month. One day, I heard she'd been at Marshall's house for a couple of nights, so I left work and raced to his home. *Enough is enough!*

I parked in the driveway, marched to the front door, and banged repeatedly. A curtain fluttered, and I heard whispers, so I increased my knocking. After a couple of minutes, Marshall answered the door. He was wearing nothing but his underwear.

"Who are you?" he asked.

"You know exactly who I am. I want to talk to Samantha."

"Samantha's not here."

I glared at him and retorted, "I'm not leaving until I talk to Samantha."

We locked stares, and finally, he hollered, "Sam . . ."

When she walked up behind him, I stepped through the door and said, "Get in the car. You're coming with me." She looked drawn. Her skin had a greenish tinge, her eyes were sunken, and her hair was completely disarrayed.

She didn't want to come with me and told me to leave her alone. So, I reached for her arm and yanked her out the door. Sam tried to retreat, but I kept a firm hold and pulled her towards the car.

"Hey, you can't do that. You can't force her to go," Marshall hollered.

"Back off if you know what's good for you," I retorted. My heart was pounding against my chest. I didn't know what I was doing, but adrenaline kept me moving forward.

When we reached the car, I opened the door and pushed her in. She didn't struggle. She slumped in the front seat and crossed her arms protectively against her chest. As I sped away, Marshall stood on his front porch, his mouth agape.

I turned towards our house. Sam's initial stupor became fury. She was screaming obscenities at me, lashing out with unthinkable names. Her words were tearing a hole in my chest, but I wasn't about to back down.

I pulled up to a red light, and when I stopped, Sam opened the passenger door and bolted. Without hesitation, I put the car in park, opened my door, and chased after her. Vehicles were honking behind me, but I didn't pay attention.

When I reached her, we struggled. I pushed and pulled her back towards the car. We were screaming at each other. Sam was hysterical because I was interfering in her life. I was vaguely aware of the spectacle we were making and briefly wondered if someone would call the police, but I kept pulling her along.

Once she was back in the car, she slumped and cried, "You don't get it. We're in love. You can't keep me away from him. We're going to move away and be together."

Somehow in all the pandemonium, her words got through. "Move away? What are you talking about?" I grilled.

She spat swears at me in reply, and just like that, the fight left me. In a much calmer voice, I repeated, "What are you talking about? Where are you going?"

Glaring, she spit out, "Marshall loves me. He's taking me to Toronto. We're going to live with his uncle. We're going to be together. You can't stop me."

"When?"

"I don't know. We're gonna drive there with his cousin."

Taking several deep breaths, I slowly and deliberately responded. "Marshall doesn't love you. Marshall is going to use you. What will you do when he's done with you and dumps you on the side of some highway? How will you get home?"

"He would never do that. He loves me!"

I didn't know what to do, so we sat in silence. After a moment, I picked up my phone and called Mike. When he answered, I told him I had Samantha and was on my way to get him.

Everything suddenly made sense. Shayna's text messages asking Sam to go to a hotel room, the revolving door of girls, and the story I'd heard about a girl passing out and waking up naked in a man's bed. They were grooming girls for sex trafficking! *How could we get Samantha to understand before it was too late?*

I picked up Mike and told him Sam was planning on moving to Toronto. Shocked and equally frightened, he tried to reason with her. Nothing we said made any difference, she was determined, and we couldn't make her see reason. We drove to Sam's grandparents, and they tried to reason with her, but she was deaf to reality. She kept repeating that they were in love and we didn't understand.

CHAPTER 24

The Sorrow
In Her Eyes

Sleep, what was that? Rolling over in bed, I lay still for a moment, my eyes tightly shut. Abruptly, I turned over and threw my face into the pillow, unable to bear the thought of another day. *Don't move. Don't think. Stay still.*

Every morning was the same. I allowed myself a brief thought. *I can't face today. I'm going to stay in bed. I can't take it anymore!* After which, I'd wearily crawl out of bed, get dressed, and head to work. Once I was there, the endless chatter of people going about their day made my skin crawl. I couldn't stomach the inconsequential noise, so I'd walk out and start my daily routine of scoring the town for sightings of Sam.

She had disappeared again. However, we knew she hadn't left the province because Marshall's court date was approaching for a theft charge. Mike and I started discussing the drastic option of having Sam placed on a seventy-two-hour mental health hold, after which we planned to whisk her to Mexico and get her out of Marshall's grasp, but we worried it would further alienate her if we didn't succeed.

On the day of Marshall's hearing, Mike sat in on the proceedings. We wanted to keep tabs on Marshall's every move and make him distinctly aware of our determination. Mike watched Marshall from the back of the courtroom and glared at him as he entered his plea. We hoped our constant presence would pressure him to give up and tell Sam to go away for good.

I lived with constant dread. My instincts told me our interference infuriated Marshall. We were in a war! I wasn't letting up; every single time I spotted Sam, I pulled up to her and saw her appearance had changed dramatically. Her eyes were bloodshot, she was terribly thin, and she swore profanities at me each time we interacted. She said horrible things, threw each sexual encounter in my face, and wished me dead. Sam seemed to relish the pain her words inflicted. Her friends were always around her, egging her on. I no longer recognized her.

However, I refused to give up. Somewhere inside the stranger in front of me, my little girl was trapped, and I'd rather die trying to find her than walk away. I started carrying a tire iron under the front seat of my car. I wanted it close at hand in case I needed to defend myself. Mike was feeling the same and had placed a baseball bat under our bed. Neither one of us discussed the subject. We didn't know what the other was feeling.

I also felt ashamed. *Damn mental illness, and damn my genetics.* I had failed my little girl. My mother had dealt with depression her whole life, and I'd battled depression, and now my baby was being pulled into a catechism, and it was my fault.

How had it come to this? I wondered. *How had we lost our daughter to a bunch of lowlives?* In my ignorance, I never thought either of our children would get involved with criminals. Arrogantly, I'd felt as many others do: *It must be the parent's fault!*

Now, we were the parents being judged and scrutinized.

As Mike and I headed home one night, I made him drive past one of the properties I knew Samantha went with Marshall. We turned the corner, and my heart leaped. For a brief second, I spotted what looked like the back of Samantha's head through the front window.

"She's there. Stop!" I yelled. Mike screeched on the brakes and asked if I was sure. Nodding, I jumped out the door before the vehicle came to a complete stop and ran towards the house.

With adrenaline pulsing, I barged in the front door. People scattered in every direction, a couple jumped out a window, and the owner, a guy in his mid-twenties, bolted out the back door, with several teens close behind. It was pandemonium. I forced my way through two teens into the kitchen, where empty bottles, half drank beers, and smoked cigarette butts littered the table. The stench of marijuana permeated the air, and a thick haze of smoke caused me to blink.

Samantha and Shayna jumped up from the living room couch, and Sam screamed at me to leave her alone. "You're coming home," I yelled back.

Marshall and three other male teens grouped together. He planted his feet firmly, puffed up, and advanced towards me. Shayna ran around me and positioned herself with Marshall. She screeched at me to leave Samantha alone.

"You can't come in here. Get out!" Marshall spat.

Violently, I threw my arms across the table. Glasses, cigarettes, and bottles flew in every direction, shattering as they hit the walls and floor. I turned to face Marshall and the others.

"Shut up, Shayna," I hissed in rage.

Marshall angrily yelled that I couldn't speak to her that way.

"I will do whatever I want," I retorted. Shayna screamed at me, and I shouted back. Samantha was crying and swearing. She said she'd never go with me.

Abruptly, I said, "You are coming home." Then, I turned and stormed out the front door and back to my waiting vehicle. Once inside, I began to shake. Mike had called the police when I went into the house, so we sat and waited.

Two officers pulled up and knocked on our window. We asked them to remove Samantha from the house. "She's in there, and they're smoking pot and drinking alcohol. An adult is supplying it."

We thought providing alcohol and drugs to minors was an offence and assumed there would be repercussions. Only, it wasn't that simple. Sadly, one of the officers leaned inside the window and explained. "The fact that an adult is on the premise is actually better; they have supervision." I was livid. *How could a grown man feeding alcohol and drugs to teenage girls be considered supervision?*

"I'm sorry there isn't anything we can do; Samantha is over fourteen."

"What do you mean? She is still a child," I wailed. "Marshall is planning to take Sam out of the province. She's a minor. What if we report her missing?" I cried.

He shook his head and said, "If he takes her out of the province, we won't be able to do anything unless he commits a crime and gets arrested. We can't go looking for her. She's just another runaway."

I burst into tears, and the officer said, "We'll get her out of the house and make her go home with you, but she'll probably leave again."

The two policemen walked to the front door and knocked. Mike and I stared at one another. No one was going to stop Marshall. What could we do if the police couldn't help us?

Samantha came out the front door, one arm in each of the policemen's arms. She was livid! "Go home with your mom and dad," one of the officers said as he opened the passenger door, and Samantha reluctantly sat down.

Sam screamed at us all the way home, and when we arrived, she threw open the car door and pounded up the front steps. Mike and I followed her inside, where she continued screaming profanities while darting back and forth like a caged animal. Abruptly, she rushed downstairs to her bedroom, then dashed back upstairs, still swearing.

She was erratically pacing, tore open a kitchen drawer, and pulled out a butcher knife, after which she ran back down the stairs and locked herself in the bathroom.

I followed her down and began repeatedly banging on the bathroom door. The water was running, and the sound of Sam's ragged breathing frightened me.

"Leave me alone!" she screamed.

"Open the door . . . *now!*" I retorted in panic. She didn't reply, so I bolted back up the stairs and back down to pick the lock.

Abruptly, Sam shoved the door open and pushed around me. She then darted to the far corner of the living room, defensively swinging the knife out in front of her.

"I'm going to kill myself," she hysterically declared.

"Give me the knife," I demanded and took a step in her direction.

Frenziedly brandishing the knife, she frantically replied, "Don't come near me, or I'll stab you."

Once more, I stepped forward; she jerked back and pointed the knife in my direction.

Her eyes were crazed, and her stance defensive, so I stopped advancing and quietly stated, "You are not going to stab me."

"Yes—I will," she screamed.

We stood opposite one another, eyes locked. In mere seconds, my mind raced through various scenarios. *I could lunge at her and wrestle the knife out of her hands. She's not going to stab me. What if she does or stabs herself?*

Again, I said, "You won't stab me."

"I will. I hate you. Just leave me alone. Go away! Leave me alone."

The pure hatred in her eyes tore at my heart. I didn't recognize her. Her eyes were black voids of emptiness. Her fury was palpable, and I realized she meant every word! The thought filled me with despair. Again I contemplated lunging at her for the knife, but I was afraid. I was terrified for her. *If she hurts me, she'll have to live with it for the rest of her life.* I pictured her sitting in jail, perhaps years in the future, and falling to pieces with the realization of what she had done. *It would destroy her.* The image stopped me in my tracks. I couldn't bear knowing my baby would live forevermore with tortured regret. I knew that behind her wrath, my little girl was lost and desperately begging for help.

Time stood still as we glared at one another. A memory crossed my mind with lightning speed. My blonde little girl was sitting in the back seat of the car as we went for a drive. Surrounded by colouring books and crayons, she was happily humming.

"I chose you guys," she said.

Mike and I laughed and asked her what she meant, and she'd replied, "When God asked me who I wanted to be my mom and dad, I chose you guys."

Time slowed down as Sam seemed to push herself as far into the corner as she could. Her hands were trembling slightly. We continued to stare at one another.

"Baby . . . please put the knife down," I pleaded.

Two police officers appeared behind me—the same two who had picked her up earlier. Mike had called them. They asked me to step aside and cautiously approached Samantha.

Although I didn't want to, I did as they instructed. Speaking in a gentle, soothing voice, one officer asked Sam to put down the knife. She refused and tried to push herself further into the corner. It felt like a long time as they both continued talking to her, and eventually, she lowered the knife.

One officer rushed forward and ordered her to turn around. Once handcuffed, they walked her out the door and placed her in the police cruiser. The tears rolling down Sam's cheeks matched the despair I felt.

Mike and I followed the police cruiser to the hospital, where the doctors took her in for observation. When we arrived, she was sitting in a separate room, and we followed her in.

As we waited for the doctor, Samantha begged me to take her home. "Mommy, please, I'm sorry. Don't leave me here, please!"

Shaking his head, Mike took my hand, squeezed it tight, and firmly told me to be strong. "We can't take her home. She's playing you."

I knew he was right, but I wanted nothing more than to hold her in my arms and make it better, the way I used to when she was little and had a scraped knee. Inside I was boiling over with sorrow, fear, and anger. *How could God let this happen? What had we done to deserve this? Why was my baby suffering the way she was?*

The medical team told us to go home. Samantha would be in for at least the night. They wouldn't conduct a risk assessment until the morning and would call us after. However, we somehow didn't get a call; instead, they discharged her. By the time I arrived at the hospital the following morning, Sam was gone.

Distraught, I demanded to know why they released her and hadn't notified us. They refused to tell me anything; they said they weren't able to discuss Samantha with me unless she gave consent.

"She's a child!" I screamed. "If she hurts herself, it's on your heads!"

The nurse on duty asked me to leave. She said I was making a scene. I was enraged. Both Mike and I had assumed they'd detain and possibly even admit her. We thought her obvious mental distress would mean a psychiatric assessment. It didn't.

We were alone—no one would help us. The police couldn't force her to stay home, and the hospital wouldn't admit her. *What were we supposed to do?*

CHAPTER 25

Wrath

Having Samantha discharged from the hospital without our knowledge incensed me. I was mad at the world. When my dad passed away unexpectedly when I was eleven, I thought that was the worst pain I'd ever experience. I'd used the grief as a measuring stick. Whenever confronted with anguish, I'd tell myself: *You can get through this, you got past Daddy's death, and this isn't as bad as that was.* What had previously given me comfort no longer worked. Nothing compared to the sorrow I was feeling.

I no longer cared about anything besides getting Samantha the help she needed and bringing her home for good. So, I checked out of my everyday responsibilities and focused on only her. I shut everyone out; there was nothing worth talking about. Whenever I did speak with someone, I found myself resenting them. Casual, mundane conversation irritated me. Sometimes, I wanted to scream at people to leave me alone!

At night, I hardly slept, and during the day, I wanted nothing more than to hide away in my bedroom. Every day was a nightmare. The pain in my chest was a physical reminder of my shattered heart, and then I started experiencing back pain intermittent with tingling numbness down my legs.

Although we didn't go to church as a family, I had always tried to be a good person. I'd never hurt anyone on purpose and wanted to be compassionate and generous with others, but what was the point if Samantha was lost? In turn, I cursed myself and my mom and grandmother for genetically passing down whatever mental anguish Sam was feeling. I hated my heritage and cursed God for allowing Sam's bullying throughout her life, for bringing Shayna into our lives, and for letting Samantha suffer the way she was. I was enraged.

At a young age, my grandmother had taught me to pray before bed, and doing so was part of my nightly routine. It was as automatic as brushing my teeth. *Why?* I wondered. *What was the point of prayer?* So, I quit praying. I didn't want to talk to a God who wouldn't help my little girl. He had betrayed me; I felt hatred towards Him.

Every night as I tried to fall asleep, I'd automatically start to pray, then stop in anger. Bitterly, I'd fight with God. "Leave me alone. I don't believe in you anymore. Why would You let this happen to Sammy? I'm finished with You, and I will not pray, so leave me alone!"

However, when I did manage to get some rest, I'd wake up praying. I was praying in my sleep. This further enraged me! *Another betrayal—how dare He continue to prod me when I repeatedly told him to leave me alone.*

The deeper my despair, the angrier I became. If the police and the medical system wouldn't help us, we'd have to find a way to get Samantha the help she needed on our own. When Karl and Samantha had been little, I had a conversation with

Diana. Now, that conversation continuously repeated itself in my mind.

"What would you do if someone hurt one of your kids?" she'd asked.

"I'd make them pay," I'd replied. It was time to make a decision. How far would I go to save Samantha?

I ramped up my surveillance of the home we'd last taken Samantha from. My surveillance included keeping tabs on Denis, the man who lived there, and Marshall. I made several unsuccessful attempts to break into Denis's house. Sometimes, I ransacked Sam's bedroom for dairies and passwords, anything I could use.

I drove up beside Marshall every time I spotted him and made sure he knew I was following him.

I searched and found someone willing to threaten Marshall and Denis. He knocked on Denis's door and warned him to stay away from Samantha.

"If Sam comes here, you're not to let her in. You are to stay away from her. Have nothing further to do with her. This is your only warning. If I hear you haven't done as I've said, I'll come back, and I won't be so nice next time. Do you understand?"

Next, he visited Marshall's home. Marshall wasn't there, but his parents were, so my friend relayed the same message and told them, "If you care about your son, you will make sure he does as I say."

Within a day, Samantha showed up at our door. Marshall and the others had told her to leave. They didn't want her around. We took her in and kept her under lock and key. I watched her every move and made sure she was never out of my sight.

By that time, I had closed down the salon. Jill had violated a non-competition agreement and opened a salon by the same name as mine in her home. So, I'd given up. I didn't have the energy to fight her and didn't care anymore.

Once Sammy was home, it was quiet for a while. Sam's friends had frozen her out, and although she was distraught, she had nowhere else to go. So, I made Samantha go to a therapist once a week. She hated going, but every Wednesday, I'd physically force her into the car.

She brooded and sulked, often lashing out, but I wouldn't give in, so eventually, she quieted down. Again, I dared to hope, but Marshall and Denis made another move within a couple of weeks and started secretly messaging her.

One night while Sam slept, I logged into her Facebook account. What I discovered incensed me. Denis had been private messaging her. His communications were flirtatious, and he was asking her to "come party."

Furious, I replied, "This is Sam's mom, and you've been instructed to stay away from Sam. This is your final warning!"

He didn't call her after that, and soon after, moved away. It was a slight relief—one less place for Samantha to hide out, one less creep in her life.

CHAPTER 26

No Turning Back

With Denis out of the picture, Marshall and his buddies were forced to find an alternate hangout. Samantha was with them again, and I was desperately trying to find her, sure the plans to take her to Toronto were getting closer.

When our presence was disturbing to Marshall and his friends, he'd get angry and tell her to go, but he always called her back. Since we couldn't reason with Samantha, we decided to look at other alternatives. Discreetly, I started asking around for someone willing to scare Marshall enough to leave without Sam.

I met with a man at a coffee house to discuss what I needed him to do. "I want Marshall hurt a little, maybe a broken leg or something like that. I don't want him killed, just scared," I said and added, "How much will that cost?"

"Look, Monika, I have no problem arranging this for you, but there are no guarantees."

I asked him to explain what he meant, and he replied, "If we go ahead, it might go as you want—he gets roughed up a little and scared enough to leave, or . . ." he shrugged his shoulder, "he might fight back, and things could get a little rougher."

"How much rougher?"

"If things get out of hand, he could end up in much worse shape than you want. Once you set this in motion, there is no turning back; he could even die. It's a possibility."

Frightened, I nodded. With tears in my eyes, I said, "I don't know what else to do, but I don't want to kill anyone."

We talked about the cost and when I wanted to put the plan in motion. Finally, I told him I needed to think it over and would be in touch. I was frightened. *There has to be another way, but what is it?*

Mike and I agonized over our next move and decided to go to court and request the seventy-two-hour mental health hold. It was a risky move. If granted, it meant she'd be arrested, kept for observation, and then released. She would be livid, so we needed to grab her and whisk her out of the country as soon as she was released. Otherwise, we'd probably lose her for good. She would never forgive us!

Time was running out. We were hearing rumours of Marshall making preparations to leave. Terrified that Samantha would go if we didn't do something fast, we made the agonizing decision to petition the courts. Mike filled out the appropriate paperwork and waited for his turn to present our request to the local judge when I frantically called him and asked him to hold off.

I had picked up Samantha and was heading home with her. Samantha looked horrible; her skin was shallow, and she was vomiting and crying. Within a couple of hours, she wasn't able to stand; throes of excruciating back and abdominal pain along with the glossiness in her eyes convinced me to get her to the hospital.

When we arrived, the same nurse I'd argued with upon Sam's previous visit was on duty. Testily, she had us fill out paperwork and instructed us to sit and wait. Hours went by, and the spasms in Sam's back increased to the point where she could no longer sit, stand, or speak. I helped her to the washroom, and as we made our way back to the waiting room, she collapsed to the floor.

"You can't let her lay on the floor!" the nurse bellowed. "She has to sit on a chair."

"She can't sit on a chair—she's in excruciating pain. She needs a bed," I retorted.

"She can't sit?" she asked.

"No," I replied.

Within a few minutes, they placed a bed beside the front desk, and a nurse helped me move Samantha onto it. "She can lay here until a doctor can see her."

By that time, Sammy was incoherent, and when they attempted to draw blood, they discovered her veins had collapsed. It took five attempts to get the needle into her arm, followed by several attempts to put in an intravenous line. She was severely dehydrated and anemic. As they poked to her, Samantha didn't move; she didn't even register what was happening around her.

Samantha's breath was shallow, and her skin was cold to the touch. I sat by the bed, holding her hand and stroking her hair. After several tests, the doctor said she had severe pancreatitis and would need to be admitted.

I slept in a chair beside her bed, anxiously fussing over her every time she moved. The following morning, the doctor said she'd be staying for a few more days because they needed to run further tests. She ended up in the hospital for two weeks. Pancreatitis can be life-threatening in severe cases, and the doctor was concerned.

For the most part, the staff was fantastic, except for one nurse. Once I walked in as she was trying to get Samantha to sit up and as Samantha struggled, she pulled her forward abrasively and spat, "Hurry it up. I don't have all day." Another time, she came in to draw blood and loudly announced, "We need more blood to test for STIs." With each interaction, she was more and more abrasive. Eventually, I intervened as the nurse berated Sam to quit whining while trying to take more blood. "What is your problem? Do your job, and stop being rude every time you come in here."

Another nurse who witnessed the interaction whispered, "You should write a formal complaint about her."

When the hospital released Samantha, we took her home feeling immense relief. The tests hadn't found a chronic disease.

CHAPTER 27

The Sound Of Silence

Samantha was fragile and spent another week in bed, but she slowly started putting weight back on and improved a little more each day. We locked her in the house, and I kept a watchful eye, fully aware she could bolt at any moment. I was a prison guard.

Once she was able, I made her resume her weekly therapy. She fought me at every turn, and again, I found myself physically forcing her. It was gruelling; I'd wrestle her into the car while she screamed profanities at me. After each session, she'd emerge emotionally drained but encouraged. Then, the next week, we'd go through the same madness.

Slowly a week turned into two, and soon, she'd been home a month. It was the longest we'd managed to keep her! However, I didn't allow myself to feel hope. Instead, I lived in constant fear. I couldn't let my guard down; every time I had in the past had proven disastrous. So I was hyper-vigilant, eager to keep her away from everyone.

When she mentioned Shayna, I deflected, hoping she'd eventually get tired of asking, but I also knew I couldn't lock her up forever. It was one day at a time!

As time went on, Sam kept improving, and then she broached the subject of going back to school. Surprised but pleased, I agreed to go with her to speak with the principal. Samantha had missed a lot of school, but the timing seemed right since a new semester was beginning.

When we left our home, Sam felt positive and hopeful, but the closer we got to the school, the more her demeanour changed. By the time we pulled up to the front doors, she was visibly shaken. We walked into the school building side by side, and Sam deflated before my eyes. Instantly, there was a visible change in her demeanour. She slouched, her eyes dropped to the floor, her breathing became laboured, and fear permeated the air.

The cafeteria went silent upon our entrance, every eye focused on us, and I experienced my own feelings. As we turned down the right hallway towards the principal's office, I felt myself tensing with anger and fury towards the bullies and the administration that had failed to stop it.

Quickly, I reached for Sam's hand and said, "Sammy, you don't have to come back here if you don't want to. In fact, I don't want you to."

"Really?" she asked.

"Yes, let's go home," I replied and together, we walked back out the doors.

Although I desperately wanted Samantha to finish school, going back there would have further damaged her psyche. I knew she'd never succeed in that environment. We would find another way!

I woke to the sound of Samantha sobbing and trembling. When I asked her what was wrong, she said, "Everyone hates me."

"Why? What's going on?" I gently asked.

"I need to talk to Shayna; I miss Shayna. Please, Mom, can I go see her for just an hour?"

I didn't want her to go see anyone, especially Shayna, but she'd been home over a month, and I was afraid if I kept her locked up much longer, she'd run away again. So, although my every instinct was telling me to say no, I agreed, "Okay, but you have to promise me you'll come home."

After setting parameters, I dropped Samantha off at Shayna's grandma's, where Shayna was staying once more, and told Sam I'd be back to pick her up in an hour.

When I went to pick up Samantha, neither girl was there. A feeling of overwhelming dread hit me. My skin went cold; I felt something was very wrong. Frantically, I dialed her number, and it went directly to voicemail. With shaking hands, I logged into her Facebook account. Her page made me gasp. Her private messages made me burst into tears.

Sammy was pleading with Marshall to forgive her for leaving. She was telling him she loved him, and he was calling her horrific names. Message upon message from Marshall told her she was worthless and threatened to beat her up.

Trembling, I dialed the police station. When an officer finally responded, the words tumbled from my mouth. I wailed my terror and said Sam was missing. I read the messages to him and begged him to look for her, but he told me he couldn't until she was gone for over twenty-four hours.

"You know who he is, please . . . please just look into it," I begged, but it was no use.

Angry, I hung up the phone and started driving. I went to all the usual places, but she wasn't there. No one was.

I didn't know what to do, so I kept checking her Facebook, looking for anything, some minor sign that she was with friends, rather than what I feared.

I drove and searched for an hour before I called Mike because I didn't want to frighten him. And I didn't want him to blame me the way I was blaming myself. During that time, I called every friend of Sam's I'd ever known, hoping someone would say they had just seen her. I dialed Shayna half a dozen times before she answered. She said she hadn't seen Sam. I wailed and begged her to tell me the truth.

"I haven't seen her—I promise," she said.

Horrified, I started going through each of her Facebook contacts, searching for their information, looking for phone numbers. Finally, I found someone with a visible number. It was a boy she'd often talked about, a boy she'd once said was Marshalls's childhood friend, and they had spoken in the morning. In the post, he'd asked her to stay away from Marshall. He seemed concerned, so I quickly dialed his number. He answered on the second ring.

"Hi, this is Samantha Proulx's mom. Have you seen her today? I'm looking for her, and I can't find her."

He told me he'd seen her by the skate park, and they'd talked for a while.

"Was she alone?" I asked.

"Yeah."

Panic struck. I told him Samantha had received threatening messages from Marshall.

"Yeah, she told me. I told her to stay away from him. He's messed! She said she wasn't gonna have anything to do with him anymore, but then I saw her talking to him," he replied.

My heart dropped with each word. *Where is she? I have to find her!* "I'm afraid," I blurted out. "I think he is going to hurt her. Did you see her go with him?"

"I don't know. I didn't see, but . . . um, she seemed fine."

"Please . . . please, call me if you see her or she gets in touch with you," I begged.

"Of course, Mrs. Proulx, I will," he promised before hanging up.

Shaking, I called Mike at work. "I can't find Sam," I began, "and I've looked everywhere. I think something might have happened to her." Afterwards, I turned left and drove towards the skatepark. *Maybe she's back there.* I thought.

Time seemed to stand still as I drove up and down our small community. Twice more, I called Shayna and asked if she'd seen Sam. She assured me she hadn't. I was nearing hysteria. *This is all my fault. I should have paid to have Marshall hurt. Why didn't I just do it? So what if he accidentally died? So what if I went to jail! I'd spend my whole life in prison to have Sammy home!*

Desperate to do something, I called Marshall's cell number. When he answered, I asked if Samantha was with him. He swore at me and hung up.

I dialed him again and said, "If she's with you, I need to speak with her now!"

"I don't know where she is; don't call me again," he replied, as random voices catcalled in the background.

I dialed his number the third time. "Listen here, you little punk. If you know where Sam is, you better tell me, or else."

He laughed at me and mocked, "Or else what? What ya gonna do?"

"If anything happens to Sam, I will hunt you down, and I will break your damn legs," I spat.

"Are you threatening me? You better watch your back," he angrily retorted.

"No . . . I'm warning you. You better watch your back," I said before the line went dead.

Never have I felt as much fear as I did while searching for her. I kept forcing the panic down; there was no time to panic. What if she was bleeding somewhere? What if she was in pain or afraid? Images of her lying in a ditch kept popping up. I cursed God for turning his back on us! I was terrified and furious.

My cell rang, and I jumped. "Hello?" I stammered.

It was the officer I'd spoken with earlier about looking for Sam, "Hi, Mrs. Proulx, we've received a complaint from Marshall Carnegie. He says you threatened him."

"I don't know what you're talking about," I coldly replied.

"Are you sure? I understand you're looking for Samantha, but you can't utter threats," he stated.

"Like I said, I don't know what you're talking about."

"Okay, then. Just don't call him again," they warned.

It was starting to get dark. Mike and I had been separately searching for Samantha for hours. Dread replaced my initial fear that Sammy might be hurt, and it was so consuming I felt physically ill. She'd been gone for hours. *Maybe, we were too late! Perhaps she was lying in a ditch, slowly dying. What if she was already dead? Where would be a good place to beat someone and dump them?* I wondered.

Mike called me. He wanted to meet up and keep searching together, but I didn't want him to know where my thoughts had gone, so I said, "I don't know; I think we should search separately. That way, we can cover more ground."

The tightness in my chest was unbearable. My composure was slipping. The desire to give in to fear and break down was rising in my throat. I drove to the walking trails. They were fairly secluded with big trees, a creek, and good coverage.

Maybe they lured her here, I thought. As I neared the walking trails, I reached under my seat and brushed my fingers against the tire iron I'd hidden for protection, then I parked and got out of the car.

With a sinking sensation in my stomach, I started walking around, dragging my feet across the ground, pushing through tall grass, searching, calling her name, crying. I was shaking, more frightened than I'd ever been in my life. *Mommy is coming, baby. Mommy is coming.*

She'd been missing for eight hours. No one had seen her. We'd searched everywhere we could think of, but there was no sight of her. Fighting the urge to scream, I got back into my car and bowed my head.

"Dear God, if You care about us at all, please don't let Sammy get hurt. Please, please, I'm so sorry for anything I've ever done. Please, I will do anything to bring her home. Anything. I need Your help now more than ever; I'm begging!" I stayed with my head down for what felt like a long time, shaking and pleading.

When Mike and I met up, he got into the car, and I moved to the passenger seat. My eyes were swollen. I could no longer think or speak. Gently, he put his arms around me and whispered, "We'll find her—I promise! We will find her."

Aimlessly, we drove around; I wasn't willing to go home and needed to know where she was. Two hours later, we finally spotted Marshall and three other guys walking about. We followed them as they darted down a back alley near Shayna's home. As they neared her house, we pulled up and parked.

Mike and I got out of the car, and I demanded, "Where is Samantha? Where is she?"

Startled, they said they didn't know, but I spotted movement in the bushes and darted forward. Samantha and Shayna were hiding under a blanket; both girls were stumbling drunk.

I ran up, pulled Samantha by her left arm, and forced her into the car. Shayna started screaming at me to leave her alone. "You said you didn't know where she was," I answered. "You lied; you knew how worried I was, and you lied anyway. How could you?"

At home that night as Mike and I lay in bed, I quietly said, "Shayna's in trouble too. I wish we could help her, but we can't—I don't have it in me. We can only save one of them, and Sammy is our baby."

"I know, hon, I know," he echoed.

CHAPTER 28

A Little Faith

Unfortunately, that wasn't the end of our ordeal. After that horrific night, Sam buckled down, and the strides we'd made the previous month broke away. If Marshall contacted her, she ran to be with him. *Where did we go wrong? Why does she love a guy who abuses her and threatens her?*

Samantha wasn't always gone. I kept pressuring her to leave Marshall for good, and sometimes she'd show up, but every time she did, she was sick. She had several stays at the hospital during that time—twice for pancreatitis attacks.

Our interactions between Sam, Marshall, and his friends continued to be volatile, and I grew paranoid. Instinctually, I felt Mike and I were in danger. Every night I'd check our door, locks, and windows repeatedly before going to bed. Sleep continued to elude me because of my worry for Sam's safety and ours but also because I was experiencing severe back pain.

My legs tingled all the time; burning heat and stabbing pain radiated from my spine to my toes. Walking was excruciating, sitting was nearly impossible, and nothing eased the constant pins and needles.

One evening, Samantha called me and asked me to pick her up from Shayna's. It was the first time she'd initiated contact, so I got in the car and hurried into town. The drive was excruciating; finding a comfortable way to sit as my right leg tingled brought tears to my eyes. I'd been ordered on complete bed rest while waiting for an MRI, but because she was out there, I went and kept pushing myself even when the pain made me crazed.

Praying, I pleaded with God to end Sam's suffering and bring her home for good. I bargained the ability to walk for her safety. "Dear God. If I have to suffer, even if I never walk again, I accept it, as long as she's safe and at home."

When Sammy got into the passenger side, she burst into tears. "I was asleep, and when I woke up, Marshall and Shayna were doing it," she blurted out. "I thought she was my friend. How could Shayna do this to me? She knows I love him. He said he loved me too. We were gonna go away together. Why would they do this?" she cried.

Seeing her hurt didn't bring me joy, but I was hopeful. I wanted their betrayal to open her eyes. I wanted it to finally keep her away from them, for the nightmare we were living to finally end.

Days turned into weeks, and Sam was still home. I was bedridden, so we watched a lot of movies together. I introduced her to my favourite comedies, and she fell in love with *Soap*. She even started smiling once in a while. It was wonderful, but still, I waited for the next time she ran. I was on edge. The anticipation of heartache was insufferable. I kept thanking God for bringing her home and committing to live with the horrific pain I felt every day. I thought it was the price He was asking me to pay.

One morning as I sat on the side of my bed, trying to muster the strength to stand, Samantha walked in and sat beside me.

"Mommy . . ."

"Yes?"

"I have to tell you something," she said with tears streaming down her cheeks.

I took one look at her and knew exactly what she was going to say, so I braced myself to hear the words and nodded.

"While I was away . . ." she began, "we used to talk about killing you and daddy."

"Uh, huh . . ."

"One night, we were sitting around, and they were talking about . . . um . . . about coming to the house . . . and doing it."

"Yeah . . ." I encouraged in a voice that sounded eerily calm. I held my breath a little, afraid to spook her into silence. She fleetingly glanced at me, then wrung her hands together before continuing. "We used to talk about it a lot, but that night was different. They kept saying, 'Let's go, let's do it tonight.' They kept asking me how I wanted to do it, and . . . and I didn't know what to do."

Hearing her detail, their plans didn't horrify me. It was confirmation of what I'd known all along, and I was glad to have it out in the open. Now that it was, I wanted to hear everything, so I kept silent and let her talk.

"Everyone was getting all excited about it, and they kept bugging me to say yes. They wouldn't leave me alone, so I told them I was too drunk. I said, 'Let's do it another night; let's party.' They were mad at me, but then we just drank and stuff."

I swallowed the lump in my throat and reached for her. She folded into my arms and sobbed as I said, "It's okay, honey. I knew. It's okay."

Sam was home a little over a month when her friend, Clara, reached out on Facebook to taunt her about Marshall. "He says he hates you; he wishes you were dead. He wants me now. He never liked you!" Her words were callously cruel. She spewed hatred.

In the past, reading Clara's repulsive words would have shocked me. That was no longer the case. I'd witnessed first-hand Marshall's ability to turn previously *good* kids into cold, heartless monsters. My only thought was to briefly wonder why so many youths lacked empathy and kindness.

Directly above Clara's jeers, there was a string of messages from Mrs. Lens. As I read them, my blood ran cold.

"Samantha Proulx is a lying little witch. Apparently, she told her mom I gave her pot."

Marshall replied by adding, "She's always lying. She should just kill herself already."

Perhaps part of the problem with youth is nasty people like Mrs. Lens, I thought as I angrily punched her number into my phone. *I should have confronted her when she smoked pot with Shayna!*

"I don't know where you're getting your information, but Samantha has never said anything about you. Samantha is not even the one you smoked pot with; that was Shayna. If you don't want kids saying you're giving them pot, don't give it to them! Now, I want you to remove your hateful posts, or I will go to the police."

Mrs. Lens removed her posts, but she had already done the damage. Sammy was curled in a ball, struggling to breathe through an anxiety attack. She'd been home, away from all those people, yet they wouldn't leave her alone. They weren't satisfied and still wanted more blood.

Again, I went on the offence, this time from my bed. I followed Marshall's every move on social media and began messaging him to leave town "for his own good."

❧

The days went on in an agonizing blur of pain. Mike and I were invited to some friends' wedding in a neighbouring town a couple of hours away, but since I was bedridden, I couldn't go. Sammy had been home for a couple of months, and she was terribly bored, so I encouraged Mike to take her as his date.

"It will do her good. She's been cooped up, and she's been really good at taking her medicine. She deserves a reward, plus it'll give you the opportunity to spend time with her. I think she could really use some Daddy time."

He agreed, and when he asked Samantha if she wanted to go, her face lit up. Excitedly, Samantha rummaged through my closet and picked a dress to wear.

They left on Saturday morning to attend the wedding, would spend the night at an old friend's home, and return Sunday. I wished them a good time and fervently hoped Sammy wouldn't get into any trouble.

The next day, they arrived much later than I'd expected. When they came home, Sammy looked radiant. She'd had a wonderful time. The wedding had been beautiful, and Sam had spent the night dancing and reconnecting with old friends, whom she hadn't seen in many years.

"Sorry we're so late getting back," Mike said. "We went to church this morning before heading out."

"Oh, church? Since when do you go to church?" I commented. Mike had never shown much interest in attending church; he claimed to be a non-believer.

Looking rather sheepish, Mike mentioned wanting to go spend the next weekend at our friend's home. "Leo and Wendy would like us to visit. We can go up Friday night, spend the weekend, and come back on Sunday."

I was reluctant. My constant pain made all movement excruciating, so I said no, but he insisted.

"I'd really like to go. Something happened to me. I don't want to tell you about it; I want to show you. You can lay on the couch the whole time; you don't even have to do anything!

It will be good for us," he persisted. Not wanting to disappoint him, I reluctantly agreed to go.

During the week, I received an urgent call from my doctor. He managed to get me in for an emergency MRI, but I needed to go immediately. He was extremely concerned about my pain level and worried I had a damaged nerve in my spine, so I gathered my bearings and went to the clinic.

The following weekend we packed up and headed to Leo and Wendy's. Sammy came with us to spent time with their daughter. It was a nice visit; they were extremely accommodating, and we spent the majority of our time watching movies and lazing about.

Saturday evening, after asking me about my MRI, Leo said, "You have to meet my pastor; come to church tomorrow."

"I don't need to go to church; I'm okay. Even if the MRI comes back with bad news, I'll accept it as long as Sammy is safe," I stated. I didn't want to go, but Mike immediately agreed, so reluctantly, I nodded.

Leo shook his head and grinned at me. "God doesn't work that way."

"If you say so," I replied while thinking *It's always worked that way for me.*

The following morning I found myself sitting near the back of the congregation, switching my position back and forth, struggling to make it through the service. As the service went on, sitting became increasingly difficult, so I stood and walked to the back of the church to brace my back against the wall for the remaining time. My right leg was twitching with terrible spasms, and every second seemed an eternity.

Near the end of the service, the pastor said, "I feel that some people here need healing. So if that person is you, I welcome you to come to the front so that we may pray together.

Oh, my, what a bunch of nonsense, I testily thought. *When will this be over soon so we can go home?*

A few people started walking to the front as I began to pace in one spot, switching the pressure from leg to leg, trying to ease some of my spasms. Briefly, a thought entered my mind, *You should go up. No, I'm not going up, no matter what. This is stupid.*

Slowly, warmth started in my chest. It was slight at first, then gradually intensified. I resisted and crossed my arms across my chest in defiance. *I'm not going*, I thought again. A gentle tugging touched my heart, and the odd sensation of being pulled forward started my feet moving towards the front. *You should go! What? No, I'm not going up front!* I tried to pull back, but the more I did, the stronger I felt the tugging sensation as an invisible string propelled me towards the front. Finally, annoyed, I threw my hands up in the air and said out loud, "Fine."

When I reached the front of the church, the pastor took my hands in hers and gently started to pray. Heat coursed through my spine as she spoke, and for the first time in months, a little of the pain eased. I walked out feeling better than I had in months and even went for a gentle quad ride with Mike and sat at the table for supper instead of propped up on the couch. The drive home was amazing; I didn't cry or wince with every bump in the road and could even sit up instead of laying back, trying to keep my back flat.

In the morning, my doctor called with incredible news. The MRI didn't show significant nerve damage. I wasn't going to need back surgery, and with time I would heal.

My healing wasn't instantaneous; there were still months before I fully recovered, but with each day, the pain lessened after that day at church. I learned to believe and trust that God doesn't expect us to bargain. Finally, I understood. He doesn't work that way!

CHAPTER 29

My Daughter—
My Hero

Like my back pain, Sammy's problems didn't disappear overnight. It was a gradual progression. Mike and I started attending church and visiting Leo and Wendy almost every weekend, and Samantha came with us. We took her everywhere, not wanting to chance her staying home, getting depressed, and possibly contacting the old crowd.

When the school year started up, we enrolled Sammy in a virtual school, and I took on the role of being her tutor. Sammy flourished with her new school. For the first time in years, she felt successful. She was able to work at her own pace, which allowed her the freedom to build upon her strengths. Her new teachers were incredibly supportive. When she had difficulty, we experimented with various teaching techniques until we found what worked for her. The result was a young lady who started to enjoy learning.

Marshall finally left, and Sammy started retreating from her relationships with all the toxic friends she once had. It was difficult for her. The more distance she put between them, the angrier they became. We blocked most peers from her Facebook account, changed her phone number, and kept her away from town as much as possible.

Permanently severing Sam's bond with Shayna was the most troublesome. Samantha still wanted contact with Shayna. We allowed it out of fear. Although we wanted Sam to completely stop seeing her, we worried pushing her to do so would cause her to leave again. With each visit, Sam returned a little less enthused. She was gradually changing!

During one of the last visits she had with Shayna, Sammy met a young man. Samantha called to ask if she could stay a little longer, and I immediately panicked.

"No. I want you home now!" I screamed.

"Mom, don't be mad. I met a guy," Sam replied.

"Oh, fantastic, here we go again—another loser. I hoped you were done with this, but I can't trust you to follow the rules," I spat. In the background, a woman encouraged Sam to hang up, but she didn't. Instead, she asked if she could invite the boy for supper.

A week later, Kyle sat down for supper with our family. Mike, Karl, and I were rough on him. We grilled the poor boy.

It must have been love at first sight because Kyle didn't give up. He kept coming back. Kyle was from a town four hours away from us, but he moved in with a friend to keep seeing Sam.

They were inseparable. Within a few months, Kyle needed a new place to live, so we let him move into the spare room in our home. We received a lot of criticism for allowing a boy to move into our home. However, we were willing to give a little to make certain Sammy stayed away from her previous friends. It's easy to be stringent with rules and judgments if you've never worried about finding your child bleeding out on the bathroom floor.

The reality of suicidal thoughts, unhealthy life choices, and manic episodes put a different perspective on what we considered important. I believe other parents whose children suffer from mental illness will understand our plight.

When Kyle moved in, Mike immediately set ground rules and demanded Kyle get a job, which Kyle did. Mike was harder on Kyle than I was; it took Mike longer to trust him. I often wondered how long it would be before Kyle decided he'd had enough. Fortunately, Kyle stuck it out, not only through Mike's demands but also through Sam's many ups and downs as she went through therapy and a number of medications.

Eventually, Sam's depression was under control. It wasn't easy on her or us! Each time a medication failed, it brought its own turmoil, and there were many failures before the success.

Also, as often happens with people suffering from mental illness, there were many times when she began to feel better and went off her medicine. Doing so *always* led to a dramatic relapse.

Sam also worked tirelessly on graduating while working a part-time retail job. Unfortunately, the predator who wanted to take naked pictures of her at Shayna's grandma's started stalking Sam at work. He wandered around the store for hours or hung around the door, waiting for a chance to speak with her. This happened until I cornered him in the store and told him to stay away. "I'm no longer *nice*. You mess with my family, and I'll mess with you!"

Samantha graduated from high school with a K&E certificate. Seeing Sammy in her grad gown brought me immense joy. My baby did it!

There were so many times I didn't know if she'd succeed or even make it through the day. However, despite all the ups and downs and the lack of educational support from previous educators, *she did it!*

We celebrated by inviting twenty people to her graduation, and watching her get the certificate was one of the best days of my life. Afterwards, we had a campfire, and Karl played guitar.

After graduating, Sammy worked in various office positions. She is orderly and approachable. People like her, and yes, she can do much more than originally expected of her. I am immensely proud to say, *they* were wrong. You can't put limits on what a person can accomplish at the age of six!

About five years ago, Shayna reached out to us. She wanted to reconnect and hoped to rebuild the relationship. Part of me still missed her, but I was proud when Sam decided against it. She said having Shayna in her life would be detrimental to her well-being. It was a brave decision and shows how much Sam has grown!

When Kyle popped the question, Sammy accepted, but the happiness also brought flashbacks. One evening, Sam broke down and revealed some of the horrific experiences Marshall put her through, including a violent sexual assault. He used her desire for acceptance as a means to control, subjugate, and abuse her. He was young but a natural predator.

Anyone who has experienced abuse understands that trauma has a way of creeping up when least expected. Fortunately, we don't have to let the past dictate our future.

Today, Sam and Kyle are happily married. She is a successful wife and a wonderful mother, daughter, and friend. It wasn't easy! The road was long and arduous, but Sam clawed her way out of despair and back to being my Sammy again. She is my daughter, my best friend, and my hero.

Even when life feels insurmountable, keep moving forward. Never give up. There is a way to the other side, *no matter what!*

IF YOU OR SOMEONE YOU KNOW
NEEDS SUPPORT

Canadian Mental Health Association
https://cmha.ca

Flying Free Ministries
www.andreafehr.com
Flying Free Ministries purpose is to empower individuals to live daily in the glorious freedom our everyday Savior Provides.

Kids Help Phone
https://kidshelpphone.ca
1 800 668-6868

Lorie Gurnett – Transformational Coach
https://www.authorloriegurnett.com/

Samantha's Law
https://en.m.wikipedia.org/wiki/Samantha%27s_Law
https://m.facebook.com/SamanthasLaw/
Samantha's Law is an advocacy initiative in the Province of Alberta, Canada, led by Velvet Martin to prevent the wrongful processing of children with disabilities by protective services when no intervention issues exist.

Soul Sisters Memorial Foundation
www.soulsistersmemorialfoundation.com

Marci Brockman
Author, Artist, Podcaster & Educator
https://marcibrockmann.com

About The Author

Monika Polefka-Proulx knows the effects of trauma. She understands how, if not addressed, it can taint every aspect of our lives. Through her writing, Monika provides hope for others struggling to move forward from past traumas.

She fell in love with books at a very young age. When her father tragically died, she was eleven years old, and the remaining family moved back to Canada after years abroad. Fitting in and relearning English was difficult for a child who had spent the previous four years only speaking Spanish, so she submersed herself in literature. Books provided solace and an escape from loneliness and shyness.

Monika has been happily married to her childhood sweetheart, Mike Proulx, for over thirty years. She is the proud mother of two amazing adults, Karl and Samantha. She loves spending time with her family, camping, and playing with her beautiful grandchildren. The family owns an automotive and autobody restoration shop and lives in Alberta, Canada.

Through determination and her love of books, she has overcome shyness, depression, self-doubt, and a crisis in faith. Her passion for writing has led her to share her experiences and expand on her desire to help others struggling with similar experiences. Books have the power to transform, heal, and allow us to escape.

FOR ADDITIONAL CONTENT
Visit: authormonikapolefka-proulx.com

Made in the USA
Columbia, SC
28 June 2021